MONEY
OF THE
BIBLE

KENNETH BRESSETT

www.whitman**books**.com

© 2005 Whitman Publishing, LLC
3101 Clairmont Road · Suite C · Atlanta GA 30329

ISBN: 0-7948-2005-0

Printed in Canada

All items illustrated in this book are genuine coins and artifacts from the collection of the author, except where noted.

Certain coin images (as noted in their legends) were provided courtesy of the British Museum, Ira and Larry Goldberg, Johns Hopkins University Numismatic Collection, Leu Numismatik, Lawrence Stack, and Kerry Wetterstorm.

Some chapter introduction photographs and other interior photographs, taken in Egypt, were provided courtesy of Sarah Waldemer (St. Louis, Missouri).

Bible-related and other illustrations were provided courtesy of Dalmatian Press, LLC.

For a complete catalog of numismatic reference books, supplies, and storage products, visit Whitman Publishing online at www.whitman**books**.com.

TABLE OF CONTENTS

FOREWORD

Biblical coins have long captured the imaginations of collectors. The desire to hold coins that circulated in the Holy Land when Jesus walked the earth, or to handle coins of later times that refer to biblical events, has always held great appeal.

Even in ancient times people avidly sought "artifacts" related to Jesus, the apostles, and saints. Christians of the Roman and Byzantine empires often wore reliquaries thought to contain fragments of the wooden cross upon which Jesus was crucified, thorns from his crown, or something related to an apostle—a fragment of bone or a piece of a relic.

Is it any wonder the desire for a tangible link to the storied days of a religion has survived the passage of time? Our world certainly has changed, but the nature of people has not.

Though the study of "biblical coins" has a long pedigree, the conclusions made of these coins have not always been correct. Sometimes this was due to the social, political, or religious agendas of an author, other times to wishful thinking or the paucity of the archaeological record when a work was published.

In modern times we are the beneficiaries of an archaeological record that has accumulated substantially since the 19th century. We are especially fortunate with coins: we need not rely on the good word and fanciful stories of a merchant, because there are many fine references available to shed light on our investigations.

Kenneth Bressett brings the whole spectrum of this field into focus in a way that marks this as something more than a coin book. Not only are the coins researched in depth, but they are placed in context within the fields of archaeology, geography, art, history, and religion. Here myths are discharged, possibilities are explored, and facts—as they are known—are revealed.

With this book we have something fresh and original that should please many readers, from the complete novice to the advanced collector. Those who are new to the field will benefit from the clarity of the text and the lavish illustrations, and experienced numismatists will enjoy Mr. Bressett's careful investigations of theories and the finer points of evidence.

We are fortunate to have this book, which is nothing less than the fruit of decades of careful study by of one of our field's most distinguished authors.

David L. Vagi
Oviedo, Florida

David L. Vagi is a specialist in Greek and Roman coins and antiquities. A staff writer for Coin World *and past editor of the* Journal of the Society for Ancient Numismatics, *Mr. Vagi is an award-winning author, teacher, and member of numerous scholarly associations. Through his company, Delphi International Ancient Art, he serves clients worldwide and is a consultant to museums, auction houses, and publishers in the United States and Europe.*

INTRODUCTION

INTRODUCTION

Countless people, places, and events are described in the Bible. They are part of a world that existed thousands of years ago at a time that was very different from today's way of life. It is not easy to relate to the culture of biblical days, and it is often difficult to understand the significance of stories that were recorded in the books of the Bible. Theirs was a much different and smaller world, without the communication, travel, and social and recreational activities that now occupy our lives.

The vast differences in customs between the ancient and modern worlds are sometimes confusing to anyone who is not familiar with the chronology of the past. Exactly when Moses, David, and Solomon lived, when and where the Exodus took place, what the world was like when Jesus was born—these are questions that many people find difficult to answer. Biblical accounts of many events often have no supporting contemporary documentation. They have been fertile ground for numerous historians, theologians, and archeologists to explore in an attempt to satisfy their curiosity about historical accuracy. The layman, however, is often left with no direct connection to the past other than what is taken on faith and assurance.

There is little written evidence to chronicle the lives of ancient individuals other than kings and rulers. Many of the cities mentioned in scripture no longer exist, and it is difficult to know with certainty when, where, or if certain wars, civilizations, events, or catastrophes actually took place. The great museums of the world have exhibits and artifacts that support and explain ancient cultures, but the majority of people never get to experience any close connection with the distant past. One of the few "hands on" activities that we can savor is the study and collecting of ancient coins that have survived to give us a direct link and confirmation of past events.

Coins touched the lives of nearly everyone thousands of years ago, just as they do today. At a time when there were no other means of mass communication, coins served as the newspapers of the day to spread the word about wars, kings, emperors, and current events. The images on ancient coins carried messages, or propaganda,

intended to educate and inform those who came in contact with them. As such, coins provide us with a running commentary on past events in a way that no other artifacts can supply. From the time that coins were first used as a medium of exchange in the middle of the seventh century B.C., until the present time, they have given us an unbroken record of world history, boundary changes, rulers, and important events.

The connection of ancient coins with biblical history is a close association that provides us with a straightforward opportunity to verify the historical accuracy of Bible accounts, and an opportunity to hold in our hands a piece of the past that was "eyewitness" to the events of the day. Unlike other museum artifacts, many ancient coins are still plentiful enough to be available at a reasonable cost to anyone who seeks them. While some of the coins shown in this book are unquestionably rarities, many other pieces can still be purchased from professional coin dealers at prices under $100 each.

A natural question here would be how such coins could have survived for millennia and still be available at any price. The answer to that is quite elementary. Even from earliest times, coins were made in large quantities for use in trade and commerce. They circulated freely and were often saved and stored by those who could accumulate wealth. However, there were no banks or investment institutions in ancient times and hoards of coins could only be secreted away and hidden until needed. Any premature death, capture, or hasty move to another locale could result in the money being left behind. In numerous cases, such hoards were left forgotten and untouched for centuries until they were discovered in modern times. Some of those coins were preserved as fresh as the day they were interred; others have suffered the ravages of time. All are important artifacts.

The most common ancient coins that are still available to collectors are copper pieces that were used for day-to-day purchases. These were coins of low value that often lasted in circulation for decades and received hard usage. They are usually found in worn condition, and today they are traded at surprisingly modest prices even though

INTRODUCTION

they are valuable historical documents. Large silver coins were generally used for major purchases, to settle accounts, and as a storehouse of wealth. The artistic quality and condition of silver coins is usually far superior to the more common copper pieces and, therefore, they are valued much more highly by collectors. Coins that are connected in some way to a well-known historical event always command an additional premium because of their special popularity.

The association of coins with past events is widely known and appreciated by archeologists and historians, but it is often over-looked by Bible students. This is despite the fact that money is mentioned many times in the Bible, and many important parables are connected with the use and misuse of money. An investigation into the coins and money of biblical times confirms the accuracy of the Bible and brings us nearer to an understanding of, appreciation for, and feeling of closeness to those stories.

Have you never wondered what the actual 30 pieces of silver looked like when given to Judas for his betrayal? Were they real coins like the ones we use today? What were they worth in purchasing power, and how could they be compared to the value of such a precious life? A clarification of these and similar queries can now be answered through the research of numismatic students who have diligently explored money of the past so that we might better understand ancient customs and the words of the Bible.

In the past, biblical archeology has been relied upon almost as a single source of information to help us understand the scriptures and people of the ancient world. Archeologists have been aided by the numismatic investigation of ancient coins, and lately, the two disciplines have come together to give a richer picture of their close association with life in biblical times. The exactness of this research not only shows the accuracy of biblical writings but also records history and sheds light on the people and places of those times in the same way that ancient clay tablets and the Dead Sea Scrolls have confirmed other biblical writings.

The accounts in this book offer you a unique journey into biblical times through the eyes of a numismatist. The quest focuses on confirming the stories, parables, and historical images that can be corroborated through examining examples of actual coins that passed from hand to hand among peoples of that time. The experience is sure to deepen your faith in and understanding of the most admired book ever written.

Kenneth Bressett
Colorado Springs, Colorado

CHAPTER 1

HOW THE BIBLE WAS WRITTEN

An inquiry into any aspect of the Bible must begin with an understanding of when and how this unique book was written. How did the stories originate? How have they come down to us? Who recorded them? Are the accounts factual? It is clear that no single person wrote the Bible. Not Moses, Abraham, the apostles, or even Jesus. It is a product of years of development and painstaking selection of the divinely inspired works of many authors. Taken as a whole, the Bible is without doubt the greatest book ever compiled, and one that touches on every aspect of humanity.

It has been said that writing is the most important of all inventions. That premise is difficult to refute when one considers what the written word has meant to civilizations of all times throughout the world. Without some system of writing and accounting, we could never have grown into the complex society of today because communication and commerce depend on a method of recording that can be understood clearly, and will endure as a permanent documentation of the many events and actions that have an impact upon our lives.

Prior to the invention of a system of recording important events, most societies relied upon oral traditions and those who could preserve specific details by committing them to memory. The information was then passed from one generation to the next, but often suffered from loss of details and accuracy.

There is evidence that some of the earliest forms of physical recording were the use of stones or pebbles that were scribed with simple lines or marks, probably to indicate the quantity of some commodity or a measure of time. Incised stones that have been dated to 8000 B.C. are thought to have been used to record a transaction that must have involved the number of livestock being traded or sold in some prehistoric transaction. Similar tallying devices made of clay were employed by the Sumerians in very ancient times and were used to record inventories of farm products and other goods.

SUMERIAN AND BABYLONIAN CLAY TABLETS

Above, top: Sumerian clay tablet, c. 2100 B.C. A typical receipt for produce that is inscribed in cuneiform writing. The ancient Sumerians are credited with inventing the system of writing that recorded some of the earliest historical events. (Actual size approximately 38 mm.)

Above, bottom: Babylonian clay tablet, c. 2000 B.C., detailing the sale of sheep in an ancient transaction. (Actual size approximately 30 x 38 mm.)

The Sumerian clay tokens made it possible for people to promise farm produce and other goods in payment of loans or taxes. When the debts were paid, the tokens were destroyed, just as a modern check or bank draft is canceled when it clears an account. Archeological evidence indicates that these tokens were common throughout the Sumerian culture, and it was but a short advancement to the development of a form of writing on similar, but larger, clay tablets that could be baked and hardened. Sometime around 3800 B.C. the script known as cuneiform evolved and replaced the crude markings on clay tokens. On the baked clay tablets, pictographic representations of abstract numbers recorded quantities and dates of transactions. The use of those clay tablet records soon evolved into the world's first writing system. The Sumerians are also credited with inventing the arch, the wheel, the division of the hour into 60 minutes, and numerous other important innovations.

Cuneiform script was written on soft clay with a wedge-shaped stylus and then baked to a hardness that turned the clay into a long-lasting document. What began as a system of keeping property and other records soon became the means of recording historical events, of expressing poetry, stories, philosophies, religious ideas, and much more. The practice was later adopted by the Babylonians and spread throughout Mesopotamia.

Evidence of writing on Babylonian clay tablets is not confined to a few isolated examples. The practice was widespread, and the thousands of examples of clay records that are still extant are the source of much of our known history of the ancient world. Within the past century, many archaeological finds have provided a rich archive of records and correspondences detailing the daily lives of people who lived in the 18th century B.C.

Clay tablets have given us a better understanding of the origins of civilization in the lands between the Tigris and Euphrates rivers and

SILVER DISHEKEL
OF BYBLOS

Silver dishekel of Byblos under King Azbaal, c. 350 B.C., with a lion attacking a bull on the obverse, and a hippocamp below a ship on the reverse. *Byblos* in English means "papyrus roll" or "book." The city of Byblos was a major exporter of papyrus for the area. The papyrus that was sold by Byblos was used to write the Bible and many other books and holy works. In time, the name "byblos" came to mean "book," and eventually the Holy Bible. (Actual size approximately 25 mm.)

shed much light on the early Semitic people. These records are especially important in the way they detail the development of trade, codes of law, and religion. From some of the translated cuneiform clay tablets, we know that the ancients paid debts in specified weights of silver or gold. The exchange unit of that time was called a shekel, which varied in standard weight over the centuries, but averaged about 16 grams.

A fortunate quality of the ancient clay tablets is their ability to endure over the centuries. The baked clay that was used is almost impervious to the ravages of time, and their inscriptions can still be read with clarity and understanding. Many of the tablets that have survived seem to be as fresh as the day they were written nearly three thousand years ago. A cache that was unearthed in 1975 in excavations at Ebla, a Middle East city in what is now Turkey, had been stored as a royal library or archive and contained nearly 1,000 pieces that were stacked vertically on wooden shelves. One significant piece in the group recorded an interstate treaty, the oldest known in history,

between Ebla and the city of Assur over the establishment of a free trade area. It included a variety of commercial and legal regulations, including some for crimes.

Other tablets in the Ebla discovery revealed an unknown language akin to the biblical Hebrew that was spoken more than 1,000 years later. One contained a vocabulary of Eblaite and Sumeric words, including an explanation in Eblaite of how the Sumeric words are pronounced. The Sumerians, who are credited with developing the cuneiform system of writing, were a non-Semitic people who flourished in southern Mesopotamia about 3000 B.C. Their influence on the cuneiform system of recording is found in the writings of the great Semitic cultures that developed in the area, blending their cultures with the Sumerian culture and giving rise to some of the oldest accounts detailed in the Bible.

OTHER FORMS OF ANCIENT WRITING

Unlike the Sumerians, who used clay, the Egyptians learned to use marsh-reed papyrus for a kind of paper that could be easily inscribed with a stylus and ink. At first they used a form of writing that was similar to cuneiform letters, but in time this was expanded to a more elaborate system that took advantage of the ease of writing on paper with ink. The Egyptians called their hieroglyphic script "the writing of the god's words" or "sacred inscriptions." The notion that writing came from a god was widespread in the ancient world and may have formed the basis for some of the reverence that we hold today for the compilation of ancient writings known collectively as the Bible.

Around 2000 B.C. Phoenicians in the city of Byblos (present Lebanon) devised an alphabetical script of some 80 signs. It was an unwieldy task for even the best scribe to use so many letters, and the system was soon abandoned in favor of the similar type of alphabetical cuneiform script of only 30 signs that was developed by the people of Ebla. Although those scripts were unrelated to present-day alphabets, the sounds were essentially in the same order as the later Proto-Canaanite, Phoenician, Hebrew, Greek, and Latin alphabets. When Abraham went to Egypt, he traveled as did all other travelers, going north from Ur, which used cuneiform, up the Euphrates River and west to the north coastal region of Syria, which also used cuneiform, then south through Canaan, and west to his final destination, Egypt, which used hieroglyphs.

By the 12th century B.C., the Proto-Canaanite linear alphabet was developing into numerous scripts. To the East, it was the basis for Arabic and Ethiopic alphabets. In Canaan, it became the Phoenician, Hebrew, and Aramaic alphabets that recorded many of the biblical

HOW THE BIBLE WAS WRITTEN

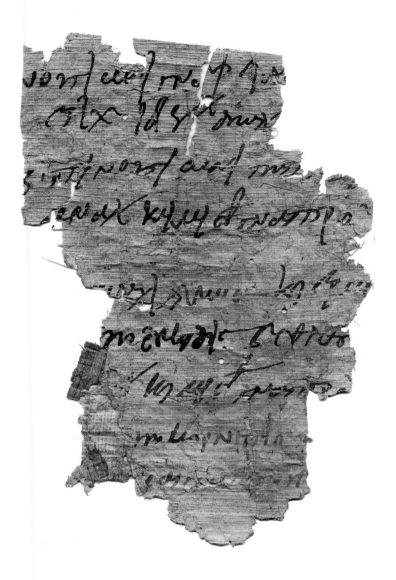

PAPYRUS LETTER

Papyrus letter recording an ancient transaction in the style of writing used by early scribes. (Actual size approximately 75 x 115 mm.)

accounts of ancient people and events. Around 1100 B.C. the Greeks adopted the Phoenician alphabet for writing their non-Semitic language and added vowels. Our word "alphabet" comes from the Greek adaptation of the first two letters of the Semitic system that they borrowed: *alpha* and *beta*.

In addition to Egyptian-reed papyrus, various other light weight writing media were used in the ancient world. These included wood, linen, leather, and parchment. They were usually inscribed with ink or paint, and while millions of such records must have been written, very few have survived because of the fragile nature of the material. Those that have come down to us include sacred literature, contracts, wills, proverbs, tales, short stories, and all kinds of receipts. As with the clay tablets, many of them were originally stored in archives and libraries, but over the years, most have been lost.

The single most important find of such documents relating to biblical history was that of the incredible Dead Sea Scrolls treasure unearthed in the ancient Judean city of Qumran in the 1940s and 1950s. The ongoing translation and analysis of the text that has been preserved on these delicate scrolls is of the utmost importance to our understanding of the original biblical manuscripts.

Among the Dead Sea Scrolls, a sheet of copper had been inscribed. On this scroll were the instructions for finding the buried valuables of the community. Known as the "Treasure Scroll," it was made of copper to ensure its preservation and survival. It had been carefully set aside and hidden so that it would be preserved for generations. Unfortunately, the key to finding the treasure has never been discovered and may remain a mystery until other pieces of the puzzle are unearthed.

Ancient inscriptions on metal were not uncommon. Silver and gold plates have been found with text relating to the Assyrian King Sargon II (c. 721–705 B.C.), and Darius I of Persia (c. 510–486 B.C). Metals used as writing materials had a special significance to ancient peoples and were often chosen for temple gifts and messages considered of the highest importance. Many ancient cultures followed this custom. One of the oldest is a Sumerian gold tablet found in Mesopotamia that has been dated to the third millennium B.C.

Nearly all of the ancients occasionally wrote on metal, but the Romans were perhaps the most prolific. The most famous metal plates in the ancient world, undoubtedly, were the 12 tablets of Roman law, which were erected in the forum of Rome in 450 B.C. In other instances, people, victories, and special events are known to have been commemorated with inscribed metal plates. Unfortunately, most of them have been melted over the years, and because of the wanton destruction, few have survived.

Roman soldiers were given their military discharge diploma in the form of a copper plate to ensure that it would never be destroyed. It was proof of their honorable discharge, and not only exempted them from further conscription, but entitled them to many privileges. Veterans were granted Roman citizenship and the right to a Roman marriage.

Stone was also chosen for writing important messages. Its strength and durability far exceeded that of baked clay tablets or the more fragile papyrus. Stone inscriptions were used extensively throughout Egypt on massive memorials and were considered particularly desirable for the perpetuation of codes of law and legal agreements, for immortalizing the deeds of rulers, and for many religious proclamations. A metal chisel and hammer were usually used to inscribe the local stones that were commonly used, particularly the soft Egyptian limestone. The Greeks and Romans preferred marble for stone inscriptions and used it almost exclusively. The oldest known stone inscription is a limestone tablet from Kish, Mesopotamia, dating to the fourth millennium B.C. Writing on stone was a widely known form of communication by the 16th century B.C. when Moses received the Ten Commandments from God.

And the Lord said to Moses: "Come up to me into the mount, and be there, and I will give thee tables of stone, and the law, and the commandments which I have written, that thou may teach them." (Exodus 24:12)

ROMAN
MILITARY DIPLOMA

Fragment of a bronze military diploma, dated to A.D. 116, for an unknown horseman of cohort II Flavia Brittonum Equitata in Moesia Inferior, under the governorship of Q. Pompeius Falco, who commanded the Legion X Fretensis as propraetor of Judaea, c. 107–110. Falco served during the reign of Emperor Trajan, and later became governor of Britain for Hadrian (c. A.D. 118–122). (Actual size approximately 55 x 60 mm.)

Documents intended to last as long as possible were engraved on sheets of metal. Gold, silver, and copper, in that order, were the most durable. The single copper sheet found among the numerous leather scrolls in the Qumran community, near the Dead Sea, offers an example of the care that was taken to preserve instructions about the location of that community's hidden valuables.

HOW THE BIBLE WAS WRITTEN

One highly significant example of a stone inscription that was found in Jerusalem, and is still available, is a proclamation of King Hezekiah of Judah dating to the year 701 B.C. It describes in detail the design of the Siloam Tunnel being dug into the mountain. Not only does it show the great accuracy of the Bible, which records the battle with the Assyrian King Sennacherib (2 Kings 18) and the digging of the tunnel, but it also answers the question of the true location of Jerusalem before the Captivity in 587 B.C.

Other records were kept on the simplest materials available to ancient people. Broken potshards were a favorite medium for writing with paint or ink. The baked earthen material was strong, long lasting, and abundant. The broken pieces of clay pottery used for writing were called *ostraca*, and were sort of like today's scratch pads. They were used for short messages, school lessons, receipts, and even voting ballots. Ostraca were used in this way as early as the second millennium B.C., and probably as late as the sixth century A.D.

A piece discovered by archeologists in 1997 contains what may be the oldest non-biblical reference to King Solomon's Temple. It records a donation to the "House of Yahweh" and is estimated to be nearly 3,000 years old. Solomon's Temple was generally believed to have been built sometime in the 10th century B.C. It lasted for four centuries until it was destroyed by Babylonian soldiers. The Bible frequently refers to the Temple by the Hebrew term "the house of the Lord," but that term has been found complete in only one inscription other than the Bible. The ostracon inscription indicates a Judean king sent it as a request to a temple contributor. It says "Ashyahu" the king commands a donation for "the House of Yahweh" of three shekels of silver. It was apparently written to serve as a receipt for what would have been approximately one and one-half ounces of silver, at a time before coins had been introduced.

The word "ostracize" comes from the practice in Athens of voting on banishment by writing an undesirable's name on a potshard. One of the most famous uses of ostraca was at the besieged fortress of Masada, where the choice of who would carry out the pact of death was decided by 10 marked shards chosen by lot. In this tragedy, hundreds of Jewish resistance fighters suffered death by their own selected members rather than surrender to the Roman army.

OSTRACON

Ostracon or potshard, c. A.D. 400, with ink inscription similar to the type of writing used to transcribe the Bible. (Actual size approximately 90 x 123 mm.)

CHAPTER 2

THE NATURE
OF THE BIBLE

CONFIRMATION THROUGH NUMISMATICS

The Bible is a historical book whose accuracy is confirmed by archeology and numismatics. It is a collection of 66 books written by 40 inspired writers over a period of nearly 1,600 years. The original manuscripts that comprise this material have been translated into modern languages many times in efforts to preserve the meaning as closely as possible to the Hebrew, Greek, and Latin texts. Scribes who copied and recopied the original scrolls were dedicated to accuracy and have provided reliable accounts of ancient testimony. Modern study and translations of the Dead Sea Scrolls provide evidence for the reliability of Jewish Scriptures in the Old Testament. Extensive writings of the contemporary historian Flavius Josephus further confirm the accuracy of biblical accounts.

Although the Bible was written by many different authors, it is consistent in its messages and interpretations of past events. Its numerous books included history, prophecy, poetry, and theology. Despite their complexity, differences in writing styles, and coverage of vast time periods, the books of the Bible agree well in theme and historical facts. Most of the ancient writings on fragile papyrus have vanished, yet many copies of original Old Testament texts have been preserved in the Dead Sea Scrolls. Some of the known New Testament manuscripts date to within 24 years after Jesus' death.

In biblical and numismatic archeology, researchers try to bring together all known facts to help us understand the scriptures better, to evaluate critical questions, and to gain a fuller appreciation of the ancient world in which the Bible was written. Countless discoveries have furnished a deeper understanding of the meaning of parables. Coins of the Roman emperors and Jewish procurators provide evidence of their existence and corroboration of their historical roles in the Bible. It is here that science and religion come together to present a richer account of the ancient world that surrounded those people and places of biblical times.

The association of coins with biblical references reaffirms that the Bible is not talking about unsubstantiated places and unverifiable events, but real people and places in history. Among the many examples that could be cited, some that stand out are the gold darics of King Darius, the Persian monarch who is mentioned in ancient texts dating to 498 B.C. and described in Ezra 4:6. Persian, Greek, and Roman coins, known as the daric, drachm, and denarius, are all mentioned in the Bible and can be clearly identified and verified by examples that are still extant. Researchers and numismatists agree that archaeological discoveries have only reinforced many biblical references. These remnants of history make clear that the stories in the Bible are about specific people and events, in a particular place and time.

THE LANGUAGE OF THE BIBLE

The original passages that are included in the Bible were written at different times and in different languages. Some were written in Hebrew, while others were in Greek and still others in Aramaic. Almost all of the books of the Old Testament were originally written in Hebrew, with the exception of the second Book of Maccabees and the Book of Wisdom. In the New Testament, all books except the Gospel of St. Matthew were Hebrew texts. The Gospel of St. Matthew was originally written in Aramaic. Many of the books of the Old Testament that were written in Hebrew were translated into Greek in the third century B.C. because the Jewish people had been living in countries where their mother tongue was all but forgotten.

The Roman *Vulgate*, written by Bishop Jerome of Delmatia in 382 A.D., was a translation into Latin from the original Old and New Testament languages. No English versions of the Bible were made until 1384, when the controversial Wycliffe Bible was published.

In the more modern translations of biblical writings, the King James Version uses words of Anglo-Saxon origin that were familiar to English readers in the 17th century. The Douay Version freely uses words of Latin origin and Latinizes the names of some of the books. Many Protestant versions, other than the King James Version, omit the Epistle of St. James.

Several versions of the Bible have been considered in this book in order to focus on the clear and precise meaning of Jesus' many parables that mention money. Sixteen of his 40 parables make reference to coins or money, and the topic is mentioned throughout the scriptures more than almost any other subject.

GOLD DARIC
OF PERSIA

Gold darics of Persia were the first coins mentioned in biblical literature. In Chronicles 1, 29:7, and later in Ezra 8:27, it is recorded that large sums of gold in the form of Persian daric coins were used to rebuild the Temple in Jerusalem. On these coins, the king is shown with a bow and spear. The reverse has only a simple punch mark. (Actual size approximately 15 x 18 mm.)

THE NATURE OF THE BIBLE

CHRONOLOGICAL OVERVIEW OF THE ANCIENT WORLD

This timeline will help in understanding the biblical and historical events of ancient times as they relate to scriptural accounts.

3000–2500 B.C. Noah. The Flood. Temple of Baal at Byblos.

Pre–4000 B.C. Prehistoric times described in Genesis.

2400–2200 B.C. Tower of Babel. Egyptian and Cretan culture.

2000–1730 B.C. Birth of Abraham, Isaac, and Jacob. Joseph sold into Egypt c. 1730.

2200–1950 B.C. Urbanization of mankind. Babylon founded.

1730–1550 B.C. Bondage in Egypt. Birth of Moses, his exile.

1400–1300 B.C. Period of Judges. 18th Dynasty Egypt and age of King Tut and Nefertiti.

1550–1400 B.C. The Exodus. Death of Moses. Joshua and the Israelites invade Canaan.

1300–1200 B.C. Trojan War. Oral tradition of *Iliad* and *Odyssey* begins. Treaty between Hittites and Egypt.

THE NATURE OF THE BIBLE

1000–900 B.C. Kings David and Solomon of Israel. First Jewish Temple built c. 995.

1200–1000 B.C. Saul made king. City of Jerusalem built by David c. 1000. Prophets Eli and Samuel.

900–800 B.C. Trade begins to flourish in Mediterranean and Near East. Prophets Elijah, Eliezer, and Elisha. King Midas.

586–323 B.C. Daniel and Ezekiel. Persian King Cyrus captures Babylon. Jews return to Israel c. 536. Second Temple built c. 515. Darius and Xerxes rule Persia. Alexander the Great conquers Israel. Socrates. Use of coinage becomes widespread.

800–586 B.C. Jerusalem destroyed. Babylonian captivity c. 587. End of First Temple Period. Palace at Nimrud. Rome founded in 753. Age of Homer. First Olympics in Greece. First true coins minted in Lydia c. 630.

323–50 B.C. Palestine seized by Ptolemy, king of Egypt, then by Antiochus of Syria. Greek becomes the lingua franca. Maccabean revolt. Pompey of Rome annexes Israel as a province in 63. Roman and Judaean coinages begin. Punic Wars. Books of Maccabees and Dead Sea Scrolls written c. 100.

A.D. 1–350. Life of Jesus. The apostles. Nero. Rome burns. First and second revolt of the Jews. Temple in Jerusalem is destroyed. Masada. Bar Kochba. Constantine the Great. Christian persecutions.

50 B.C–A.D. 1 Age of Julius Caesar, Cleopatra, Mark Antony, Herod, Pontius Pilate. Birth of Jesus of Nazareth. Augustus and Tiberius Caesar rule the Roman Empire.

A.D. 350–1000. Talmud is completed. Old and New Testaments incorporated into the Bible. Byzantine Empire flourishes. Birth of Mohammed in 622. Crusades initiated.

CHAPTER 3

COMMERCE BEFORE COINS

COMMERCE BEFORE COINS

It is difficult for us to comprehend a society when there was no money or medium of exchange. The world as we know it today could not function without a complex monetary system. We all use some form of money every day. It is involved in every life and every transaction. We all use checks, coins, bank drafts, paper money, and credit cards without thinking about why this is our money, or why it is valued at the amount we believe it to be worth. There was, of course, a time when none of this existed, and the concept of using credit cards would have been as strange to primitive man as his world of trading seems to us today.

The transfer of goods from one person to another is as old as mankind and must have been an important part of even the most primitive society. A skillful toolmaker soon learned that it was to his advantage to trade his products to the hunters that could provide him with food. Cattle, grain, and ornamental beads were found to be desirable trade items in early prehistoric times. Those exchanges must have been measured only in the desirability and immediate needs of those who traded, and quite likely varied from transaction to transaction. The concept of uniform values did not arise until there was accumulated wealth that could be stored in some form and traded even for nonessentials.

Wealth in the form of crops or livestock was the usual mark of a successful trader, but there was always the danger of loss by spoilage and sickness. It was also often impossible to trade sheep or cattle for items of a much lesser value. Consider the problem of making change for a lamb that might require half a chicken, two doves, and a small utensil. The difficulties of trade by barter soon required the use of some kind of promissory agreement that could be repaid at a later date with an accumulation of goods. There was also the problem of establishing the relative values of items that were being traded. Something that might seem to be of great value to one, might not be so to another.

Commodity money, which served civilization from the earliest of times, continued to be used in some societies up to the present. Even the current U.S. tax forms ask the question of value received in the form of barter. Much of Europe during a large part of the Middle Ages lived on a basis of barter rather than a money economy, and in colonial America, "country pay" was the common, and usual, medium of exchange among rural people. For 3,000 years Egypt, had no coins, and though ingots and rings of precious metals may have served the purposes of money in negotiations between kings and great merchants, money was practically unknown to the ordinary people.

In a well-developed and open economy, the use of money, that is to say, a commonly accepted medium of exchange, becomes indispensable. Acceptable forms of money must be something that has been widely agreed upon as being of stable value, recognizable, transportable, durable, and easily divisible. Over time the very useful metals, gold, silver, and copper, became the most popular choices, being the ideal media that could be used in nearly every transaction. These items were obviously a good choice because those precious metals have served this function well for thousands of years.

Money, as a medium for the exchange of goods, requires some notion of "property," as a measurement and value, and some conception of the way in which both parties can benefit by exchange. These three conditions were neither natural nor easy for primitive man, and the transition from trade and barter to the sophisticated use of coins and credit was a long and difficult passage. Over the ages, many things have served as money. Different societies have used items as diverse as hide-scrapers, beads, shells, stones, and tusks. In biblical lands, however, the evolution was generally quite straightforward with precious metals always being the first choice as money that was almost universally accepted.

The need for some convenient units of precious metal became widespread as trade expanded throughout the ancient world, and in time small lumps of gold and silver, or items made of gold, silver, and copper became generally acceptable in trade. The metals that were used were not pure, but often combined with other metals as found in nature. The regular combination of gold and silver, known as electrum, was the metal of choice and the most valuable prior to the advent of refining methods. Copper, or the alloy known as bronze, was perceived as being a valuable metal because it was so useful in fabricating a multitude of popular items.

Among the earliest known forms of metal used as a medium of exchange are bronze ingots from the second millennium B.C. in the shape of cast fillets approximately 10 inches long and 2 inches wide. Similar silver and gold strips were apparently also used, and are known from hoards of small pieces that were cut from the strips. In biblical lands, metal in this form was measured in the unit called a shekel. The term referred to a specific weight, and was used to quantify many diverse commodities long before the beginning

COPPER BRACELET
OF LURISTAN

Jewelry in the form of bracelets and rings was commonly traded as objects of value in the
first millennium B.C. In Luristan (Iran), this copper bracelet, decorated with lion's head
terminals, was a popular item. (Actual size approximately 62 mm.)

of coins. Quarter, half, and two-thirds shekel weights are frequently mentioned in the Old Testament, as in 1 Samuel 9:8: "Behold, I have here at hand the fourth part of a shekel of silver; that will I give to the man of God, to tell us our way."

In addition to raw metals and ingots, fabricated items were also held to be of great value. The most important of these were jewelry and ornamental items that seemed to have been coveted by all classes of people. Rings, bracelets, chains, and earrings were as popular 4,000 years ago as they have been ever since.

The first such mention of wealth in the Bible was in Genesis 13:2 where Abram (later called Abraham) is described as being "very rich in cattle, silver and gold." Abraham's wealth is again mentioned in another passage from Genesis (24:1–38) that tells of how he sent his servant to find a wife for his son Isaac. Upon encountering Rebecca at the well, he gave to her a number of precious items to win her favor:

> **When the camels had finished drinking, the man took out a gold ring, a half shekel in weight, which he fashioned on her nose, and he put on her wrists two gold bracelets weighing ten shekels.**

He also said, in Genesis 24:34–38, 53,

> **I am Abraham's servant. The Lord has blessed my master abundantly so that he has become a rich man. He has given him flocks, herds, silver, gold, men and women servants, camels and asses.**

> **The servant brought forth silver articles, and gold articles, and clothing, and he gave them to Rebecca; and to her brother and to her mother, precious things.**

In ancient Egypt, at the time of the Genesis saga, similar items were used as money and a store of value and wealth by the nobility. Common laborers and slaves had little use for money and were usually paid in grain and other necessities of life. Coins that came into use in the seventh century in other regions were not extensively used in Egypt until the Alexandrian era in the fourth century.

An early reference to the Egyptian concept of wealth is seen in Genesis 41:42 as follows:

> **Then the Pharaoh said to Joseph, "I give you charge of the whole land of Egypt." Taking the signet ring from his own hand, he put it on Joseph's. He dressed him in linen robes, and put a chain of gold around his neck.**

Details from a tomb in Thebes, circa 1400 B.C., show an Egyptian weighing large metal rings against lamb-shaped weights. Bronze rings similar to those in the paintings have been found in the region and are believed to be a form of currency from that time period. Other rings of gold or silver have also been attributed as being a similar form of currency used in trade. The very few Egyptian monetary gold rings that are still in existence are consistent in decoration and form, but vary in size, and would have been valued according to their weight.

Gold earrings and bracelets that are prevalent throughout the ancient world were decorative items that represented the wearer's wealth and status, but could also be used as money whenever necessary. Clothing ornaments made of gold were also a popular form of adornment among the rich prior to a more convenient means of storing their money. In Exodus 32:2, Aaron said to the Israelites:

> **"Have your wives and sons and daughters take off the golden earrings they are wearing, and bring them to me."**

Then in Exodus 32:24,

> **And I said to them, "Who has gold?" They broke it off, and gave it to me, and I cast it into the fire and fashioned a molten calf.**

In the Book of Numbers (3:50) we read, "of the firstborn of the children of Israel Moses took the money, a thousand three hundred and sixty-five shekels, according to the shekel of the sanctuary." Job 42:11 contains the following passage: "every one gave him a piece

GOLD CLOTHING ORNAMENT

Gold ornaments were fastened to clothing as decorations and often used as money when the need arose. This piece, in the form of a reclining winged bull with a man's head, was made in the sixth century B.C. When Cyrus allowed the Jews to return to Jerusalem and rebuild their temple, they gave their ornaments to be melted and used to build the city and temple. A piece this size and weight was equivalent to two Persian silver sigloi, or 1/16 of a gold shekel. (Actual size approximately 30 x 23 mm.)

GOLDEN SYMBOLS OF WEALTH AND STATUS

Left: Golden earring or nose rings, like this one weighing 1/4 shekel, have been cherished jewelry for thousands of years. (Actual size approximately 17 mm.)

Right: In ancient Egypt, large rings of precious metal were used as payment in place of coins. This gold ring with decorated ends is attributed to the second millennium B.C. (Actual size approximately 32 mm.)

of money, and every one a golden ring." And in Jeremiah 32:9–10, it is written, "I bought of Hanameel, mine uncle's son, the field which is in Anathoth, and weighed him the money, seventeen shekels of silver. And I subscribed the writing, and sealed it, and took witnesses, and weighed the money in balances."

MONEY THAT REBUILT THE HOLY TEMPLE

Solomon's temple was the center of worship for the kingdom of Judah from the time it was built around 1000 B.C. until it was virtually destroyed by Nebuchadnezzar of Babylon when he captured the city of Jerusalem in 587 B.C. At that time its gold, bronze, and silver furnishings were taken to Babylon and held there for the next 50 years. When the Persian king Cyrus allowed the Jews to return from Babylon to Jerusalem in 538 B.C., he gave them permission to rebuild Solomon's temple. He also returned some of the gold and silver objects that Nebuchadnezzar had taken from the temple. When Cyrus ordered the temple construction in Jerusalem, he also decreed that everyone should contribute their silver and gold to the rebuilding:

> Let (the Israelites) go up to Jerusalem which is in Judea, and build the house of the Lord the God of Israel: he is the God that is in Jerusalem. And let all the rest in all places wheresoever they dwell, help him every man from his place, with silver and gold, and goods, and cattle, besides which they offer freely to the temple of God. (Ezra 1:6)

Although this construction, which was completed in 515, was during a time when coined money was making its appearance, the Israelites were more accustomed to the Babylonian use of trade and bullion transactions. The Book of Kings 17:1–8 emphasizes that: "the children walked in the ways of their Assyrian captors, and worshiped strange gods." As such, it would not have been

unusual for the Jews to use Persian and other gold ornaments to adorn their clothing, and for them to have earrings, bracelets and rings of precious metals. They must have used these items as "money" and trade items, just as they used the coins of the kings Cyrus and Darius in a somewhat later period.

> And how he gave them the law that they should not forget the commandments of the Lord, and that they should not err in their minds, seeing the idols of gold and silver, and the ornaments of them. (2 Maccabees 2)

> And the Lord said to Moses: Say to the children of Israel "Thou are a stiff necked people; once I shall come up in the midst of thee, and shall destroy thee. Now presently lay aside thy ornaments, that I may know what to do with thee." So the children of Israel laid aside their ornaments by Mount Horeb. (Exodus 33:5–6)

Gold clothing ornaments (a Persian equivalent of buttons) were very likely among the items committed to the Temple building fund. These were the pride of those who could afford to display their wealth and their allegiance to the Persians. They were often made in the form of "strange gods" that the Jews had come to accept. A typical ornament had an eyelet on the back so it could be sewn onto clothing. It is easy to imagine that hundreds of similar things went into the melting pot, along with the rings, bracelets, earrings, and vessels that filled several baskets. In 2 Kings 1 the passage states, "Ye daughters of Israel, weep over Saul, who clothed you with scarlet in delights, who gave ornaments of gold for your attire."

These, and hundreds of other similar passages in the Old Testament, describe the use of barter, trade, gold, silver, and other items of value that were used as a form of money in ancient times. Nowhere are coins actually mentioned in any place prior to their appearance in the seventh century B.C. The occasional use of coin-like terms that have been used in some early Bible quotations are always those of translators attempting to relate unfamiliar expressions with words that might be familiar to contemporary readers. The frequent use of the word "shekel" is a prime example of something that did not become a coin until the middle of the first century A.D.

OLD TESTAMENT MONEY, WEIGHTS, AND MEASURES

Dram. 1. *Adarkon* (Hebrew). (1 Chronicles 29:7. Ezra 8:27.) 2. *Drakmon* (the Persian Daric). (Ezra 2:69. Nehemiah 7:70, 71, 72).

Piece of Money, Piece of Silver. Greek *Argurion*. (1 Samuel 2:36). This may mean coined or uncoined metal.

Bekah. Hebrew *Bek'a*. (Exodus 38:26). Equal to half a shekel.

Gerah. Hebrew *gerath*. (Exodus 30:13. Leviticus 27:25. Numbers 3:47). 1/20 of a shekel.

Maneh. Hebrew *maneh*. (Ezekiel 45:12). Equal to 50 shekels.

Pim. Hebrew *pim*. (1 Samuel 13:21). Two-thirds shekel.

Rebah. Hebrew *rebah*. (1 Samuel 9:8). Quarter shekel.

Shekel. Hebrew *sheqel* or *sela*. (Exodus 21:32, and others). There is the shekel of the sanctuary (Exodus 38:24) and the shekel of the king (2 Samuel 14:26). Their relative weights are unknown.

Talent. Hebrew *kikkar*. (Exodus 25:39 and frequently). A weight equal to 3,000 shekels of the sanctuary. Also rendered as talent of the king, talent of gold, and talent of silver. Greek *talantos*. In the New Testament.

Money of account, for which there was never a coin issued, is mentioned in a few biblical passages, but the talent has never been precisely valued. In terms of silver, it seems to have been 750 ounces, 3,000 shekels in gold, or 6,000 Greek drachms. It varied greatly with time and place. Fifteen talents of silver were equal to one talent of gold. The maneh was equivalent to 50 or 60 shekels.

In some translations, the word "sicle" is used instead of "shekel," as in Numbers 18:16, "and the redemption of it shall be after one month, for five sicles of silver, by weight of the sanctuary. A sicle hath twenty obols."

CHAPTER 4

COINS OF OLD TESTAMENT TIMES

The earliest actual coins mentioned anywhere in the Bible are the gold darics of the Persian King Darius I, who ruled from 510 to 486 B.C. After 486, the successors to Darius issued similar gold darics, and silver sigloi, with the image of a bearded kneeling archer holding a spear and bow, and an oblong incuse punch mark on reverse. The daric is specifically identified in 1 Chronicles 29:6–8.

> Then the heads of the families, the leaders of the tribes of Israel, the commanders of thousands of hundreds, and the overseers of the king's affairs came forward willingly and contributed for the service of the house of God five thousand talents and ten thousand darics of gold, ten thousand talents of silver, eighteen thousand talents of bronze, and one hundred thousand talents of iron.

In Ezra 8:26–27, we read the following:

> I consigned it to them in these amounts: silver, six hundred and fifty talents; silver utensils, one hundred; gold one hundred talents; twenty golden bowls valued at a thousand darics; two vases of excellent polished bronze, as precious as gold.

Prior to the conquest of Lydia by the Persians, few coins were used by the Persian kings. As Persia expanded west, it found a need for the use of the medium of exchange that had been implemented around 550 B.C. by King Croesus of Lydia, and his successors. In addition to being remembered for his legendary wealth, Croesus should be equally famous for his innovation of issuing corresponding coins that were made of nearly pure gold and nearly pure silver. Previously, coins were often made of a natural mixture of the two metals that is known as electrum. The difference in value between gold and silver was the influential factor in separating them into two distinct coins. Curiously, the design used on these early coins was often the same for both metals. The practice of using diverse coinage metals was continued by the Persians thereafter, and in other countries ever since.

By the end of the sixth century B.C., the knowledge of how to mint and use coins had spread to all of the important Greek cities in the Mediterranean area. Merchants from every part of the Greek world used coins in order to facilitate the exchange of goods. Not all communities minted their own coins, and many depended on the use of coinage from other districts. The Israelites had to wait several centuries before their economy and government was strong enough to support the responsibility of issuing their own coins. In the period prior to their independence, the Jews were often compelled to use the money of their subjugators and that of foreign lands. During those times, they were forced to accept coins that they found offensive because they usually displayed graven images, and often those of local gods. The reluctance of Jews to use heathen money was rooted in their adherence to Bible decree quoted in Exodus 20:1, 4, and 20.

> Then God delivered all these commandments: "You shall not carve idols for yourselves in the shape of anything in the sky or above or on the earth below or in the waters beneath the earth. Do not make anything to rank with me; neither gods of silver nor gods of gold shall you make for yourselves."

Silver coins of the neighboring districts of Aegina, Athens, and Corinth were well known throughout the ancient world, and were certainly known to Jewish traders, although none of them is mentioned specifically in the Bible. The so-called "tur-

SILVER HALF STATER AND SILVER SIGLOI

Above: Silver half stater of Lydia, 561–546 B.C., issued by King Croesus (who is still famous for his remarkable wealth). His coins were the first to be made of either silver or gold, rather than a mixture of the two metals. (Actual size approximately 17 mm.)

Below: Silver sigloi of the Persian Empire were not mentioned in the Bible as coins, but they have the same designs and chronology as the gold darics. In Ezra, the Persian king Artaxerxes, c. 465–425 B.C., supplied thousands of pounds of silver, much of which may have been in the form of these coins. (Actual size approximately 13 x 16 mm.)

tle" coins of Aegina that were first made around 550 B.C. are thought to be the earliest European silver coins. Those of Athens, made soon after, circulated widely and were a standard trade unit for centuries. They depicted the head of Athena on the obverse, and her sacred bird, the owl, on the reverse. Almost equally famous were the "colts" of Corinth that depicted a helmeted head of Athena on one side and the winged horse Pegasus on the other.

Many other coins were made and used throughout the numerous districts mentioned in the Old and New Testaments. It seems likely that most of them were familiar

A MENAGERIE
IN ANCIENT SILVER

Left, top and bottom: Some of the oldest silver coins were made on the island of Aegina where their famous silver "turtles" were used as bullion for international trade. Staters made as early as 525 B.C. show a sea turtle, and segmented punch mark on the reverse. (Actual size approximately 20 mm.)

Middle, top and bottom: The famous "owls" of Athens circulated throughout the ancient world around the middle of the fifth century B.C. when this attractive early-style tetradrachm was created. (Actual size approximately 25 mm.)

Right, top and bottom: Silver staters of Corinth circulated freely throughout the ancient world. They were known as "colts" because of the design showing Pegasus, the legendary horse that was stabled near the city. (Actual size approximately 22 mm.)

ARADOS SILVER DRACHM

The city of Arados in Phoenicia issued this silver drachm in 161 B.C. It could have circulated in Jerusalem just prior to the time the Jews were allowed to make coins of their own. (Actual size approximately 16 mm.)

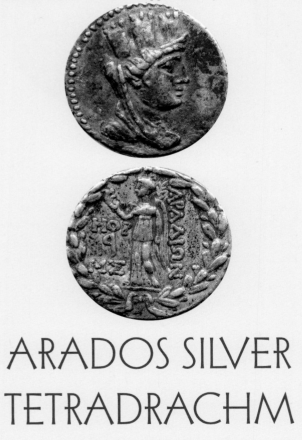

ARADOS SILVER TETRADRACHM

Silver tetradrachms of Arados were valued at one shekel each at the time this piece was made in 80 B.C. (Actual size approximately 28 mm.)

to those who handled large sums of money and needed to convert one weight system to another when making a transaction. The most commonplace would have been those pieces from the districts closest to Palestine where the shekel and its fractions was a standard for many coins. Coins from Aradus, on the northern coast of Phoenicia, were popular from about 500 B.C. until the mid-first century B.C.

> **And when Moses had gathered the multitude together again, he ordained that they should offer half a shekel for every man, as an oblation to God; which shekel is a piece among the Hebrews, and is equal to four Athenian drachmae.** (Antiquities 3.8.2)

Silver money from the Phoenician cities of Tyre, Byblos, and Sidon were also familiar to the Jews. Large tetradrachms, or shekels, and half shekels from Tyre were coins that were regularly used as offerings in the Temple, and the only silver coins acceptable in the Temple for paying the annual temple tax during the first century B.C. and later. They were readily available in the area and were of full shekel and half-shekel weight. The fact that they featured an image of the Phoenician god Melkart must have been seen as secondary to the need of a coin that was made of good silver and was the full weight as prescribed for the holy offering. In the Talmud, Tosephta Kethuboth 13, 20, it states: "Silver, whenever mentioned in the Pentateuch, is Tyrian silver." The Tyrian shekel is referred to by name at one point by the historian Flavius Josephus:

> **He then bought up all the oil, paying Tyrian coin of the value of four Athenian drachms for four amphorae and proceeded to sell half an amphora at the same price.** (War, 2.21.2, 592)

The coins of the neighboring Phoenician district of Sidon were also familiar to the Jews and were probably used for many years in large commercial transactions. The Phoenicians also used the shekel as a measure of weight, and produced coins of one and two shekel sizes, as well as a number of smaller fractions. Some attractive two-shekel coins of Sidon that were made in mid-fourth century B.C. show the figure of a Persian king in a horse-drawn chariot that is followed by an Egyptian attendant. Other similar pieces show the same scene with a different type of attendant. Both seem to be propaganda pieces attesting to some now forgotten fortunes of war.

During the brief period from about 375 to 333 B.C., the first true Jewish coins were struck. It cannot be determined if they were authorized by the Jewish High Priest or some local Persian governor.

The coins were crude, tiny silver pieces with the Hebrew inscription "Yehud," the Aramaic name for Judaea. Some of the pieces imitated the coins of Egypt or Athens with an owl on the reverse; others made use of a lily and eagle. These coins—rare today—must have

DOUBLE SHEKELS OF SIDON

Left, top and bottom: The coins of Sidon must have been familiar to the Jews in mid-fourth century B.C. for their use as international trade silver. This large double-shekel piece shows the Persian king in a chariot with an Egyptian attendant. (Actual size approximately 30 mm.)

Right, top and bottom: Some of the double-shekel coins from Sidon show the king of Persia in a chariot with a Phoenician attendant. These large coins could only be used for major purchases as they represented more than a week's pay for most workers. (Actual size approximately 26 mm.)

TYRE DIDRACHM

Tyre, in Phoenicia, made these silver didrachms c. 332–275 B.C. Such coins were valued at one-half shekel and may have been used by the Jews as temple offerings. (Actual size approximately 20 mm.)

BYBLOS 1/8 SHEKEL

Silver coins produced in the Phoenician city of Byblos in the fourth century B.C. were as small as this 1/8 shekel denomination. Despite their small size, they were equivalent to half a day's pay for a common laborer. (Actual size approximately 11 mm.)

TYRE HALF SHEKEL

Phoenician coins of Tyre, minted from 126 B.C. to 65 A.D., were accepted in the Temple as offerings because of their full weight of pure silver. The standard design shows a head of Melkart, and an eagle on a prow. (Actual size approximately 21 mm.)

been very limited in the quantities struck, and possibly intended to be more symbolic than for the convenience of trade.

Judaea remained a province of the Persian Empire until 332 B.C., when Alexander the Great made himself master of the area, as he moved to conquer what was nearly the entire known world at that time. The profound influence that his amazing conquests had upon his vast empire resulted in the spread of Greek culture, language, and, of course, the coins that he issued to accommodate trade and commerce. In time it became necessary, and customary, for Jews to use coins of Alexander and his successors as their primary monetary unit. The transition was an easy one because the standard coinage of Alexander was based on a silver drachma that was equivalent to one-quarter shekel. His tetradrachm, the most common trade coin of the day, was a four-drachma silver piece that equaled one shekel in weight.

Alexander III (the Great) of Macedon ruled from 336 to 323 B.C. Under his governance, the Jews were treated well and prospered. He founded a Jewish colony in Alexandria, Egypt, and it is from scholars in that settlement that we have received the Greek translation of the Old Testament that is known as the Septuagint, or "Version of the Seventy." The cordial relations that existed between Alexander and the Jews can be traced to a friendly visit he paid to them in Jerusalem. There he was met by Juddua the High Priest, who read to him from the Book of Daniel where it states that a Greek would destroy the Persians (Daniel 7:6; 11:3; 8:3, 20–22). Alexander rejoiced in believing this meant himself, and looked favorably on the Jews and their religion.

After the conquest of Persia, great quantities of its gold darics and silver sigloi were melted by Alexander and used to make his own coins. This was the custom in the various countries he subjugated, and the reason for his extensive coinage bearing the head of Hercules (some say it is Alexander's portrait) on one side, and the seated figure of Zeus on the other.

The gold staters that Alexander and his half-brother Philip issued had a helmeted head of Pallas Athena on the obverse and a winged figure known as Nike on the reverse. Some of these coins were struck in Palestine, Joppa, Acre, Sycamine in Caesarea, and Scythopolis in Samaria. All are biblical place-names, and evidence of the extensive use of Alexandrian coinage by the Jews, despite the inclusion of graven images that must have seemed offensive to them.

Alexander died while he was still a young and successful leader. The Jews had cause to mourn his passing and the turn of events that placed them under new subjugation. Upon Alexander's death in 323 at age 33, his empire entered a state of civil war among his ambitious generals, or successors, who fought over and divided the kingdom among themselves. The people of the Holy Land were soon pushed back and forth between two of Alexander's

PRE-CHRISTIAN COINS
LARGE AND SMALL

Left, top and bottom: From about 375 to 333 B.C., tiny silver coins were made by some Jewish authority. They imitate coins of other nations, but are crudely made, and often show designs on only one side. The inscription "Yehud" found on some of them is the Aramaic name for Judaea. (Actual size approximately 10 mm.)

Middle, top and bottom: The coinage of Alexander the Great of Macedonia was in use throughout his vast kingdom, which included the Holy Land that he liberated from the Persian Empire in 333 B.C. His silver tetradrachms were the same weight as a shekel. (Actual size approximately 27 mm.)

Right, top and bottom: Gold staters of Macedon were used in trade throughout the ancient world and were likely an acceptable form of money for any large transactions mentioned in the Bible. (Actual size approximately 19 mm.)

PTOLEMY I
TETRADRACHM

Ptolemy I of Egypt gained control of the Holy Land after the death of Alexander in 323 B.C. He issued silver tetradrachms with his portrait on one side and an eagle on the other. (Actual size approximately 27 mm.)

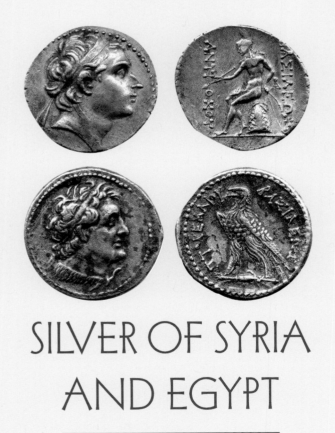

SILVER OF SYRIA
AND EGYPT

Top pair: During a rivalry between the Egyptian and Syrian kings, the territory of Palestine passed to Antiochus III of Syria, whose portrait is shown on his silver tetradrachms. *Bottom pair:* Ptolemy V of Egypt, who was unsuccessful in his efforts to retain control of Palestine and the Holy Land, was defeated in 198 B.C. by Antiochus. (Actual size approximately 28 mm.)

generals. They came under the rule of the Ptolemies of Egypt during the third century B.C., and later became subjected to the Seleucid kings of Syria.

With Syria under the Seleucids, to the north, and Egypt, ruled by the Ptolemies, on the south, Palestine was in the midst of constant bickering and warfare between two former realms of Alexander. In 198 B.C., the Syrians under Antiochus III defeated Scopas, the general of Ptolemy V, at Panium, in North Palestine, and Judaea passed definitely to the Syrians. Flush with success, Antiochus swept through Asia Minor seizing cities and provinces that had once been Seleucid. Rhodes, Pergamum, and many of the captured cities appealed to Rome, which responded in 190 B.C. by utterly routing Antiochus and his Syrian army at the great battle of Magnesia.

Throughout this turmoil, Palestine remained under Syrian control, and even prospered under the relaxed edicts of Antiochus III, who rescinded the taxes on Jerusalemites and even contributed to the Temple. He also granted Jews the right to live according "to their ancestral laws." All of this changed abruptly when Antiochus IV came to power in 175 B.C., and the Jews began to learn the meaning of his wrath. Antiochus appears to have vented his vexation upon the Jews by adopting a policy of breaking the power of their priesthood, despoiling their Temple, and substituting the worship of Zeus for that of Jehovah.

In suppressing the Jews, Antiochus IV intended to foster Greek culture and religion among his subjects. The results were quite the opposite. His coins use the title "Epiphanes" or "God Made Manifest," but his contemporaries referred to him as Antiochus Epimanas, "the mad." Among his many insults to the Jews, he burned the Torah, and defiled the Temple by sacrificing a sow upon the altar, in an effort to make the Jews conform to the Greek way of life.

The wicked Jason sent from Jerusalem sinful men to carry three hundred didrachmas of silver for the sacrifice of Hercules.
(2 Maccabees 4:19)

Offenses to the Jews continued through 167 B.C. when King Antiochus looted the Temple, killed thousands of Jews, and sold thousands more into slavery. Many of the citizens of Jerusalem fled in fear; others refusing to abandon their faith went into hiding. It was at this time that Judas, the son of a priest called Mattathias, led a revolt against the king, who was soundly defeated in 164 B.C. by Judas and his brothers, known as the "Maccabees."

There is little good that can be said of King Antiochus IV except that were it not for the stunning victory of the Jewish resistance fighters, Judaism, as it is known today, might be very different. After the

ANTIOCHUS IV
SILVER TETRADRACHM

Silver tetradrachm of Antiochus IV, the Greek king of Syria, 175–164 B.C. Antiochus looted the Temple treasury, destroyed holy texts, and defiled the altar by sacrificing a pig, in an effort to Hellenize the Jews. He only succeeded in igniting the Maccabean Revolt, which ultimately granted a degree of freedom for the Jews. (Actual size approximately 33 mm.)

ANTIOCHUS IV COPPER

Seleucid King Antiochus IV issued large copper coins with the head of Zeus and an eagle as part of a series of Egyptian-style coins struck to commemorate the defeat of the Ptolemies. (Actual size approximately 35 mm.)

ANTIOCHUS VII TETRADRACHM

A turning point in Jewish independence came when Syrian King Antiochus VII granted permission for the Jews to coin money in their own name. Silver tetradrachms of Antiochus show the king's portrait on coins he minted from 138 to 129 B.C. (Actual size approximately 30 mm.)

Maccabees recaptured Jerusalem from the Syrians and cleansed and rededicated the holy Temple, it was a time for celebration. The original festival must have involved distributing the spoils of war that would have included coins of Antiochus. The largest of them were the silver tetradrachms, or shekels, with the portrait of the king on one side and the seated figure of Zeus on the other. Minor copper coins were probably given to children. The event is still remembered today in the custom of giving gifts of coins, called *Hanukah gelt*, each year during the feast of Hanukah.

COINS OF THE MACCABEES

In the relatively peaceful century following the rebellion, the Jews were granted authority to mint coins of their own. Under the reign of Syrian King Antiochus VII, a decree was issued to Simon the High Priest that has been recorded in the First Book of Maccabees 15:6–7 as follows:

> **And I give thee leave to coin thy own money in thy country. And let Jerusalem be holy and free, and all the armor that hath been made, and the fortresses which thou hast built, and which thou keep in thy hands, let them remain to thee.**

The first coins struck under this edict were small bronze pieces issued in Jerusalem by John Hycarnus I, as a vassal of Antiochus VII, around 132–130 B.C. John was the son of Simon the Maccabee, and the nephew of the revolutionary hero Judas Maccabee. On the obverse is a lily, an often-used flower decoration for the Temple and priestly robes. The reverse shows an upside-down anchor, as it would be stored on a galley ready for use. The name of Antiochus in Greek is on either side of the anchor. The persistent use of the anchor during the next 100 years of coinage referred to the importance of the seacoast cities of the Holy Land.

Following this Jewish/Seleucid issue, the first extensive issue of Jewish coins was minted in Jerusalem from 130 to 104 B.C. by John Hycarnus I, as High Priest. These were small bronze pieces known as prutot and lepta that most often featured a double cornucopia adorned with ribbons, and a pomegranate in the middle. On the other side is the Paleo-Hebrew inscription "Yehohana the High Priest and the Council of the Jews," surrounded by a wreath.

The prutah (plural, prutot) was a small bronze coin hardly any larger than a small fingernail. The lepton (plural, lepta) was equal to one-half prutah. Lepta were usually about the same diameter as prutot, but thinner and about half the weight. During the Hasmonean (or Maccabean) period, the Greek silver drachma seems to have been valued at 336 lepta or 168 prutot. The shekel was valued at 384 prutot. The Roman denarius was estimated to be worth

96 prutot. Their exchange rate, however, varied somewhat according to their size, state of preservation, type of transaction, and a moneychanger's commission if that was included.

Judah Aristobulus I (104–103 B.C.) was the oldest son of Hyrcanus, and is reputedly the first Hasmonean to use the title "king," but none of his coins expresses that. Designs used on his coins are nearly identical to those of his father, with a double cornucopia on the obverse and a Hebrew inscription on the reverse.

Bronze prutot and lepta of Alexander Jannaeus, the younger brother of Judah Aristobulus I, were issued from 103 to 76 B.C. On the obverse of the most common types is an anchor with "King Alexander" in Greek. The reverse has a star of eight rays, and sometimes has Hebrew letters between the rays or around the outside. A much scarcer coin of his displays an anchor and lily. The famous "widow's mite" described in the New Testament parable could have been any small bronze coin, but it most likely was one of Alexander Jannaeus because his coins were so prevalent at the time.

Bronze prutot were also minted by John Hycarnus II. In 67 and 63 to 40 B.C., John was engaged in a civil war with his brother Aristobulus II, and sought the aid of Pompey the Great of Rome. Then Pompey besieged Jerusalem, defeated Aristobulus, and installed John as the "ethnarch" or ruler of the people. The design used on his coins is similar to those of John Hycarnus I, with the double cornucopia, and Hebrew inscription within a wreath.

The real ruler under Hyrcanus II had been Antipater. When Antipater was made procurator, Herod, though only 25, obtained the government of Galilee. After the death of Julius Caesar in 44 B.C., Herod at first supported Cassius, but when Mark Antony went to Syria in 41 B.C., and sought his favor, Herod was eventually made king of Judaea.

Mattathias Antigonus initiated several changes in the coins that he issued during his short reign from 40 to 37 B.C. His Hebrew name is only shown on his prutah coins, and the pomegranate between the double cornucopiae is replaced by an ear of barley. He issued two larger denominations that can be compared in value with the Seleucid chalcous and dichalcous. He was also the first Jewish ruler to depict the holy vessels of the Temple of Jerusalem on his coins.

Mattathias was the son of Aristobulus II. He attempted to rule with the aid of the Parthian King Orodes II, allegedly through gifts that included 500 Jewish women. Mattathias, with help from the Parthian army, occupied Jerusalem and laid claim to the office of High Priest. Herod I (called the Great), who was governor of Galilee at the time, fled to Rome to enlist support and was officially designated King of Judaea. Herod and the Roman legions besieged Jerusalem, and captured it in 37 B.C. The ensuing execution of Mattathias brought an end to the Hasmonean dynasty.

THE FIRST JEWISH COIN

The first coins minted for Jerusalem were small Syrian coppers with a lily on one side and an anchor on the reverse. (Actual size approximately 14 mm.)

EARLY JEWISH PRUTAH

Bronze prutah of John Hycarnus I, 130–104 B.C., with an inscription indicating he was high priest and head of the council of the Jews. Hycarnus built a sound foundation for the new Judaean kingdom. (Actual size approximately 14 mm.)

VARIOUS COINS OF
THE MACCABEES

Left, top and bottom: Judah Aristobulus I proclaimed himself king, but he remained in power only from 104–103 B.C. He was the eldest son of Hycarnus I and issued bronze prutot of the same design as his father. (Actual size approximately 14 mm.)

Second, top and bottom: Several different types of small bronze coins were made by Alexander Jannaeus, 103–76 B.C. The most common of these has a star of eight rays, sometimes with letters between the rays or near the rim. The obverse shows an inverted anchor. His bronze lepta are most likely the tiny "widow's mite" of Bible fame. (Actual size approximately 15 mm.)

Third, top and bottom: Bronze prutot, or two-lepta coins, were minted for John Hycarnus II who ruled in 67 B.C. and again from 63–40. He was engaged in a civil war with his brother Aristobulus II during much of that time, before he was installed by Pompey the Great as "ruler of the people." (Actual size approximately 14 mm.)

Right, top and bottom: Mattathias Antigonus initiated several changes in the coins he issued from 40–37 B.C. On some of his bronze prutot, an ear of barley replaces the pomegranate between the double cornucopia. (Actual size approximately 14 mm.)

COINS OF HEROD AND ORODES II

Left, top and bottom: Herod I, the Great, was governor of Galilee from 40 to 4 B.C. A man without mercy, he had two of his sons and his wife executed, and ordered the mass murder of all Jewish male infants anywhere near Bethlehem, where he heard a future king of the Jews would be born. He issued many different bronze coins. The largest was an eight prutah showing a helmet on the obverse and a tripod and bowl on the reverse. (Actual size approximately 22 mm.)

Right, top and bottom: Silver drachm of Orodes II, 57–38 B.C. When Parthian King Orodes II was victorious in a battle against the Romans in 53 B.C., Mattathias sought his aid in occupying Jerusalem. The alliance, however, was short lived because Herod and the Roman legions recaptured the city and executed Mattathias. (Actual size approximately 24 mm.)

SILVER DENARIUS OF POMPEY

During the dispute over who would rule Judaea, both Aristobulus and Hycarnus appealed to Pompey for support. It was Pompey who had brought Syria and Palestine under Roman control and occupied Jerusalem in 63 B.C. Silver denarii of Sextus Pompey showing his father's portrait on the obverse. (Actual size approximately 19 mm.)

SILVER DENARIUS OF AUGUSTUS

When Octavian defeated Mark Antony in 31 B.C., he became master of the Roman world. In 27 B.C., Octavian was given the title "Augustus," the name by which he is best known. Silver denarii, similar to this piece with his portrait, were minted until his death in 14 A.D., and used throughout the provinces during the time in which Jesus was born. (Actual size approximately 19 mm.)

In the first century B.C., the Greek empire gradually fell to the Romans. Corinth was taken in 146 B.C. and Athens in 86 B.C. Julius Caesar conquered Gaul, and Pompey brought Syria and Palestine under Roman control, and then occupied Jerusalem in 63 B.C. Both Aristobulus and Hyrcanus appealed to Pompey for support; Pompey was quick to enter into Jewish politics and decided in favor of Hyrcanus. At that point, warfare broke out anew between followers of the brothers, but ended when Aristobulus and his two sons were carried off to Rome and paraded through the streets in disgrace.

In 58 B.C., a special Roman silver denarius was struck to commemorate the defeat, by Pompey's general Marcus Scaurus, of the Nabethean King Aretas III, who supported Hyrcanus II in his battles against his brother, Aristobulus. The design shows the Arabian King Aretas kneeling in an attitude of submission. A similar Roman commemorative coin was issued in 54 B.C. to proclaim the capture of Aristobulus and his submission to Rome. The design on that coin shows a bearded Jew kneeling beside a camel, yielding to Rome by extending a symbolic palm branch.

After Syria became a Roman province, Pompey appointed Aulus Gabinus as proconsul of Judaea, and in 57 B.C., Gabinus then reinstalled Hyrcanus as high priest of Jerusalem. He also worked to suppress the revolts and introduced important changes in the government of Judaea. One of his reforms was the issuance of silver tetradrachms that were made in imitation of the familiar coins of the former King of Syria Philip Philadelphos. The new coins were distinguished only by special dates and symbols, and continued to be issued for a period of about 30 years.

The Romans brought law, order, and stability to the nations they ruled. Peace was maintained by garrisons of soldiers, whose presence was not generally appreciated. Foreign legions were stationed in Palestine, and there were heavy taxes to pay. The atmosphere was highly charged and revolt, especially where the Jewish religion was concerned, was a constant danger. In 31 B.C., Octavian, later known as Caesar Augustus, became the first ruler of the Roman Empire. It was during his reign that Jesus Christ was born.

COINS OF EMPIRE AND OCCUPATION

Left, top and bottom: Roman denarius of M. Aemilius Scaurus, who was sent by Pompey in 64 B.C. to settle the dispute between the warring Maccabee brothers. The surrender in 62 B.C. of Aretas III, the Nabataean King, was commemorated by this coin issued in 58 B.C. (Actual size approximately 18 mm.)

Middle, top and bottom: This Roman denarius was minted by Aulus Plautius in 54 B.C. to commemorate the defeat of King Aretas. The inscription "Bacchius Judaeus" refers to Aristobulus, who made his submission to Pompey. (Actual size approximately 18 mm.)

Right, top and bottom: Silver tetradrachms imitating those of the Syrian King Philip Philadelphos were issued during the Roman occupation of Jerusalem. The coins of Aulus Gabinius, 57–55 B.C., and his successors can be distinguished by a monogram near the leg of Zeus on the reverse, and distinctive dates in the exergue. (Actual size approximately 26 mm.)

CHAPTER 5

COINS IN THE NEW TESTAMENT

COINS IN THE NEW TESTAMENT

The final Old Testament issue of tiny Jewish bronze prutah coins was made by Herod the Great, who ruled from 40 to 4 B.C. Numerous designs were used on the coins made during his long reign. They can be divided into two groups: those that are dated and those that are not. The dated coins all bear the same date, the year 3. This would relate to the year of his reign, which began in 40 B.C., and would equate to 37 B.C. All the legends on his coins were in Greek, and no Hebrew legends appear on any of the coins of the Herodian dynasty. The denominations of his coins were 8, 4, and 2 prutot, and a number of small bronze prutot and lepta.

Emblems on Herod's coins included a tripod, prow, caduceus, pomegranate, shield, helmet, palm branch, eagle, anchor, and cornucopia. The wide selection of types was an indication that Herod did not want to offend the religious feelings of his subjects. The inscriptions show his name and title.

Herod was not known as "the Great" during his lifetime. He favored Greek culture, but was a man of violent jealousies and passions. He murdered his wife Mariamne and his sons Alexander and Aristobulus. He married 10 wives in all. He was cruel and tyrannical, feared and respected by men and nations. Typical of his atrocious cruelties was the murder of all but two members of the Supreme Council when he became king.

Among his undertakings were the restoration of the temple of Jerusalem, and the city of Samaria, which he called Sebaste. Some believe that the temple was built to satisfy his artistic rather than his religious instincts. He expanded a small town on the seacoast to a great city known as Caesarea and is credited with introducing Greek games to his subjects. He was also very much involved in the biblical account of the Nativity.

And when he had gathered all the chief priests and scribes of the people together he demanded of them where Christ should be born. And they said unto him, "In Bethlehem of Judaea for

---

thus it is written by the prophet." **Then Herod called the wise men, inquired of them diligently what time the star appeared. And he sent them to Bethlehem, and said, "Go and search diligently for the young child; and when you have found him, bring me word again that I may come and worship him also." The wise men followed the star and reached the manger. They fell down and worshipped him, and when they opened their treasures, they presented unto him gifts; gold, frankincense and myrrh. And when they were departed, behold the angel of the Lord appeared to Joseph in a dream saying, "Arise, and take the young child and his mother, and flee into Egypt...for Herod will seek the young child to destroy him."** (Matthew 2:1–13)

When Herod heard of the birth of an infant that some said was destined to become King of the Jews, he ordered the death of all male children up to two years of age.

[Herod] sent forth and slew all the children that were in Bethlehem and in all the coasts thereof, from two years old and under, according to the time which he had diligently inquired of the wise men. (Matthew 2:16–18)

It was because of this that Joseph and Mary fled to Egypt to save the life of the newborn Jesus. They remained there until Herod died, before returning to the land of Israel.

But when they heard that Archelaus did reign in Judaea...he turned aside into the parts of Galilee; and he came and dwelt in a city called Nazareth. (Matthew 2:22–23)

BRONZE COINS OF HEROD

Above: Bronze two-prutot coin of Herod I, the Great, showing a tripod table flanked by palm branches. (Actual size approximately 18 mm.)

Below: Bronze prutah of Herod I with his inscription on the obverse and an anchor on the reverse. (Actual size approximately 13 mm.)

These accounts of the birth and early childhood of Jesus are at odds with the chronology of that time. It is clear that Herod died in 4 B.C., and thus the Nativity must have occurred prior to that. Exactly when remains a mystery, but the best assumption places the event between what we commonly consider 7 and 4 B.C.

SILVER AND BRONZE
COINS OF AUGUSTUS

Left, top and bottom: Antioch. Silver tetradrachm of Augustus dated year 28, which equates to 4/3 B.C. (Actual size approximately 26 mm.)

Right, top and bottom: Antioch. Bronze coin of Augustus made in 5/4 B.C., near the time of Jesus' birth. (Actual size approximately 23 mm.)

COINS IN THE NEW TESTAMENT

COINS OF THE YEAR THAT JESUS WAS BORN

Some coin collectors have wondered if any coins could be traced to the year zero, or if indeed there is a year zero. The answer to both questions seems to be no. The calendar, as we know it today, turned from December 31, 1 B.C. to January 1, A.D. 1—those dates having been arbitrarily assigned to correspond with what was once widely believed to have been the birth year of Jesus. The general use of such dating was not employed until sometime around the sixth century, and no year zero was assigned to the time-line. The customary use of Christian dating on coins did not begin until 1234, and then it was used only very occasionally until around the year 1500.

What, then, was being used for money at the time and place of the birth of Jesus? To answer that, we must consider what was available in the district around Judaea in the period close to 6/5 B.C. One must also bear in mind that coins at that time were usually traded by weight, with little regard for when or where they were made. Thus, it would not have been uncommon for any coin from neighboring districts to be passed in circulation. Old Hasmonean coppers were probably the

coin of choice, and the more recently made coppers of Herod must have been prevalent throughout the district. Larger Roman copper, bronze, and silver coins would have been used in commerce and to pay necessary taxes. None of those coins, however, was ever dated in a way that was specific to the year of the Holy Birth.

One of the coins that can be dated close to the beginning of the Christian era is a silver tetradrachm of Antioch in Seleucia and Pieria. It was struck in year 31 of the Actian Era, and corresponds to 1 B.C./A.D. 1. The date consists of Greek letters with the numeric values of 1 plus 30, in that order. Greek cities that used the Actian Era started their calendar on September 12, 31 B.C., the date when Octavianus (Octavian) defeated Mark Antony in the sea battle at Actium in northwestern Greece. The coin struck 31 years later was made on the eve of what we now calculate as the beginning of A.D. 1.

Tetradrachms of this same design were issued in other years and the year 27 and would relate to the Christian calendar year of 5/4 B.C. The split-year reckoning is a result of their year beginning and ending on months that were other than January and December as in the modern cycle. Those coins were minted about 400 miles away from Bethlehem but are the closest of any to the time and place where Jesus was born.

A second, somewhat similar coin, also made in that same district of Seleucia and Pieria under the emperorship of Augustus, is a copper piece about 23 mm in diameter. The inscription on this coin also dates it to the year 27 of the Actian calendar, or precisely 5/4 B.C., which could have been the very year of the Nativity.

The large silver shekels of Tyre that were approved for use as temple offerings were also dated with years that can be translated into dates that correspond with modern Christian reckoning. All of the Tyrian coins have dates that begin in 126/125 B.C. and continue almost uninterrupted until the time of the first Jewish revolt against Rome in A.D. 66–70. Curiously, only a few of them are specifically dated to the decades just before or after the beginning of the Christian era. Those that were made after 17 B.C. seem to have been minted in Jerusalem rather than Tyre.

ENROLLMENT AND THE STAR OF BETHLEHEM

And it came to pass that in those days there went out a decree from Caesar Augustus, that the whole world should be enrolled. This enrolling was first made by Cyrenius (Quirinius), the governor of Syria. And all went to be enrolled, every one into his own city, and Joseph also went up from Galilee, out of the city of Nazareth into Judea, to the city of David, which is called Bethlehem; because he was of the house and family of David, to be enrolled with Mary his espoused wife, who was with child. (Luke 2:1–5)

COINS IN THE NEW TESTAMENT

"AND ALL WENT TO BE ENROLLED..."

The census ordered by Roman Emperor Augustus was for the purpose of taxation. Joseph would have paid two silver denarii, like this one of Augustus minted c. 15 B.C. (Actual size approximately 19 mm.)

COINS IN THE NEW TESTAMENT

The census, or enrollment, that was ordered by the Roman Emperor Augustus was for the purpose of taxation throughout the kingdom. This was the event that caused Joseph and Mary to go to Bethlehem. It is likely that the half-shekel tax would have been a Tyrian coin, or two silver denarii, which were the equivalent in Roman money. Likely candidates for the type of coins that might have been used would be any of the silver pieces made by Augustus after he became emperor in 27 B.C.

There is no actual historical confirmation of the incident that Luke describes, and his is the only extant source of information on this subject. Yet, other known records of the existence of Quirinius as a ruler in Syria, and similar enrollments in other cities, nullify the problems raised by the conflicting account given by Jewish historian Flavius Josephus of a corresponding (second) census in A.D. 6.

The journey to Bethlehem and the birth of Jesus as recorded in Matthew 2:1–13 were heralded by a magnificent star that led the Magi (Herod's "wise men from the East") to that site. Exactly who the Magi were, and even their exact number, is shrouded in mystery. Some accounts portray them as kings or princes; others say they were magicians or priests from the sacred cast of the Medes. If they were kings, we should be able to verify their existence through coins, but as of now that does not seem possible. There is no way to accurately trace their journey, or determine who they were, or their place of origin. Equally mystifying are their gifts of gold, frankincense, and myrrh. We can only surmise that the gold would have been in the form of coins, and quite likely the still-plentiful staters of Alexander the Great.

One recurring speculation holds that two of the Magi can be tentatively identified, and that they did issue coins that are well known to collectors. The first of these involves Gaspar, who is recognized as being the Indo-Greek King Gondophares, who ruled from A.D. 20 to 60. His coins show a bearded portrait of a man who would have been much younger when he made the journey to Bethlehem.

A second identification has been suggested that links the Nabathean King Aretas and his son Malichus to the Magi. One or both of them could easily have made the 60-mile trip from the Arabian city of Nabathea to Bethlehem. Aretas IV ruled from 9 B.C. to A.D. 40. His son Malichus could well be the elusive Melchior, who legend names as one of the Magi. Copper coins of King Aretas show his portrait on one side and an inscription in Aramaic on the other.

Aramaic was the common language of the Galilean region and the language that Jesus spoke throughout his lifetime when he preached or spoke to friends. He would have used Hebrew in conversations with religious leaders and when reading in the synagogue. His name in the Aramaic language was *Yeshua bar Yosef* (Jesus son of Joseph).

That the Magi believed a star led them on their journey is clear from the words used in Matthew 2:2. Rationalists have proposed that it was not a star, but a comet. Others say it was a conjunction of planets Jupiter and Saturn (7 B.C.), or Jupiter and Venus (6 B.C.); or it may have been a stella nova, a star that suddenly increases in magnitude and brilliance and then fades away. The event, whatever it may have been, was never recorded on any coin with certainty. It was not unusual to include stars or comets in ancient coin designs, but this famous occurrence seems to have been neglected.

COINS OF
THE MAGI?

Left, top and bottom: It would have been a short journey for King Aretas IV and his son Malichus to travel from their home in Nabataea to Bethlehem. Speculation is that Malichus could have been the prince, or future king, identified in early German literature as Melchior of the Magi. The bronze prutah of Aretas minted during his reign from 9 B.C. to A.D. 40 show the king and queen. The inscription on the reverse is in Aramaic, the language of Jesus. (Actual size approximately 20 mm.)

Right, top and bottom: Indo-Parthian King Gondophares, 20–60 A.D., may have been one of the Magi who traveled to Bethlehem. He is shown on his copper coins minted many years after the Nativity. (Actual size approximately 12 mm.)

COINS IN THE NEW TESTAMENT

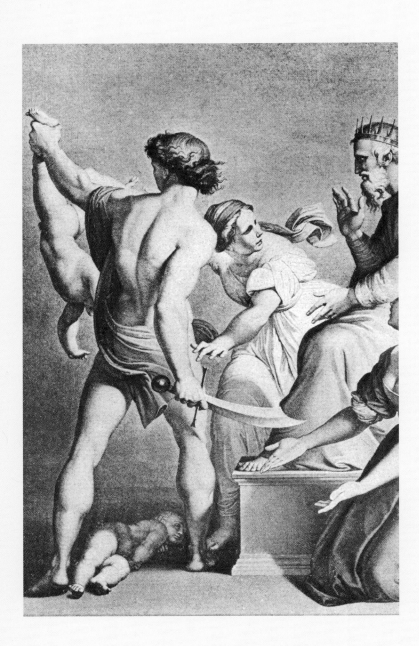

HIGH PRIESTS FROM THE ACCESSION OF HEROD THE GREAT TO THE DESTRUCTION OF JERUSALEM

Appointed by: *Herod the Great*
1. Ananel
2. Aristobulus
3. Jesus, son of Phabes
4. Simon, son of Boethos
5. Matthias, son of Theophilos
6. Joazar, son of Boethos

Appointed by: *Archelaus*
7. Eleazar, son of Boethos
8. Jesus, son of Sie

Appointed by: *Quirinius*
9. Ananos (Annas)

Appointed by: *Valerius Gratus*
10. Ishmael, son of Phabi
11. Eleazar, son of Ananos
12. Simon, son of Camithos
13. Joseph (Caiaphas)

Appointed by: *Vitellius*
14. Jonathan, son of Ananos
15. Theophilos, son of Ananos

Appointed by: *Agrippa I*
16. Simon Cantheras, son of Boethos
17. Matthias, son of Ananos
18. Elionaios, son of Cantheras

Appointed by: *Herod of Chalcis*
19. Joseph, son of Camithos
20. Ananias, son of Nedebaios

Appointed by: *Agrippa II*
21. Ishmael, son of Phabi
22. Joseph Cabi, son of Simon
23. Ananos, son of Ananos
24. Jesus, son of Damnaios
25. Jesus, son of Gamaliel
26. Matthias, son of Theophilos

Appointed by: *the people during the war*
27. Phannias, son of Samuel

PROCURATORS OF
JUDAEA, 3 B.C. to A.D. 66

Those with asterisk are the only ones known to have issued coins.

1. Ethnarch Archelaus
2. Coponius* (served under Emperor Augustus)
3. Marcus Ambiuius* (served under Emperor Augustus)
4. Annius Rufus
5. Valerius Gratus* (served under Emperor Tiberius)
6. Pontius Pilate* (served under Emperor Tiberius)
7. Marcellus
8. Cuspius Fadus
9. Tiberius Alexander
10. Ventidius Cumanus
11. Antonius Felix* (served under emperors Claudius and Nero)
12. Porcius Festus* (served under Emperor Nero)
13. Albinus
14. Gessius Florus

These were the men who governed in the Holy Land during the first century after the birth of Christ. Much of the daily life of the Jews was controlled by religious or government dictates. A number of religious groups or sects developed throughout the area. Most Jews did not belong to any sect, though those who did were widely admired. Among those sects were the Pharisees (the largest sect at the time of Jesus), the Hasidim (the "pious ones"), the Zealots (who refused to pay taxes to Rome), the Essenes (who possibly wrote the Dead Sea Scrolls), and the Sadducees (most of whom were members of the family of priests). The rabbis were teachers who interpreted the law and applied it to everyday life.

The procurators who ruled in Judaea governed under Roman authority. Not all of them issued coins, and few of them are remembered historically other than those mentioned in biblical text, or who were known to have issued coins. Pontius Pilate is the most famous because of his role in the trial of Jesus. Antonius Felix and Porcius Festus were governors during the trial of Paul.

HERODIAN COINS
OF THE FIRST CENTURY A.D.

Herod Archelaus (4 B.C. to A.D. 6)

Herod Archelaus became ruler of Judaea upon the death of his father, Herod the Great. Raised and educated in Rome, the title Ethnarch was confirmed upon him by Augustus. As the only prince

COINS OF
A HATED PRINCE

Bronze prutot of Herod Archelaus, 4 B.C. to A.D. 6, varied in size and design. This son of Herod I ruled so harshly that he was hated by the Jews and removed from office by Augustus, who banished him to Gaul. (Actual size approximately 17 mm.)

of Judaea so named, his coins can be attributed to him with certainty. He ruled over the districts of Judaea, Idumaea, and Samaria. His coins are all undated and bear mainly maritime emblems, such as the prow, galley, and anchor. Other types feature the double cornucopia, a helmet, or a bunch of grapes. The main denomination was the prutah, but a double prutah was also issued.

When Joseph and Mary learned of the death of Herod the Great, they returned to the land of Israel. A reference to this incident is found in the New Testament.

> **When Herod had died, behold, the angel of the Lord appeared in a dream to Joseph in Egypt and said, "Rise, take the child and his mother and go to the land of Israel, for those who sought the child's life are dead." He rose, took the child and his mother, and went to the land of Israel. But when he heard that Archelaus was ruling over Judea in place of his father Herod, he was afraid to go back there, and because he had been warned in a dream, he departed for the region of Galilee, and came to dwell in a city called Nazareth.**
> (Matthew 2:19–22)

Herod Antipas (Tetrarch of Galilee, 4 B.C. to A.D. 40)

Herod Antipas began to issue coins only after he founded and settled his new capital called Tiberias. His coins are all dated and were issued in several years beginning in A.D. 19/20, thus attesting to his long reign. Antipas was Herod the Great's original heir, but owing to disputes a change of will gave him only Galilee and Paraea. The emblems on his coins are all of flora such as the reed, the palm branch, a small bunch of dates, and a palm tree.

> **At that time Herod the tetrarch heard of the fame of Jesus.** (Matthew 14:1)

> **He replied, "Go and tell that fox, 'Behold, I cast out demons and I perform healings today and tomorrow, and on the third day I accomplish my purpose.'"** (Luke 13:32)

Antipas is the Herod who is so often mentioned in the New Testament and was called "that fox" by Jesus. He was the person who ordered the execution of John the Baptist at the request of his wife,

Herodias, after her daughter by an earlier marriage, Salome, had pleased Antipas with a dance. Pontius Pilate sent Jesus to Antipas when he learned Jesus was a Galilean.

> **But when Herod's birthday was kept, the daughter of Herodias (Salome) danced before them, and pleased Herod.** (Matthew 14:6)

> **For Herod himself had sent forth and laid hold upon John and bound him in prison, for Herodias' sake, his brother Philip's wife; for he had married her...and when the daughter of the said Herodias came in and danced, and pleased Herod...the king said unto the damsel, "Ask me whatsoever thou will..." and she came in... and asked saying, "I will that thou give me by and by, in a charger, the head of John the Baptist."** (Mark 6:14–27)

COIN OF "THAT FOX" HEROD

Herod Antipas ruled under Tiberius and is mentioned in the Bible in several places. Jesus referred to him as "that fox" in Luke 13:32. (Actual size approximately 19 mm.) (Photograph courtesy of Leu Numismatik)

Jesus was sent to Herod Antipas by Pontius Pilate when he found that he was a Galilean. Because of former disputes, Pilate was not on good terms with Herod. When the transfer of Jesus to the jurisdiction of Herod was made, the old quarrel with Pilate was ended. The incident is described in Luke 23:7:8 as follows:

> **Upon learning that he was under Herod's jurisdiction, he sent him to Herod who was in Jerusalem at that time. Herod was very glad to see Jesus; he had been wanting to see him for a long time, for he had heard about him and had been hoping to see him perform some sign.**

Herod Philip I (4 B.C. to A.D. 44)

Herod Philip I is the least well-known son of Herod the Great. He was the first Jewish ruler to include his portrait on any coin, but the scarcity of his issues makes them elusive for collectors to acquire. His rejection of the Mosaic Law against "graven images" was carried further by the inclusion of a representation of a Roman temple on the reverse of most of his coins. His coins were dated from the year 5 to the year 37 of his reign, though not all dates occur.

> **Now in the fifteenth year of the reign of Tiberius Caesar, Pontius Pilate being governor of Judaea, and Herod being tetrarch of**

COINS IN THE NEW TESTAMENT

BRONZE HERODIAN COINS
OF PHILIP AND AGRIPPA

Left, top and bottom: The portrait coins of Herod Philip are all quite rare. Luke (3:1) identifies him in the Bible as tetrarch of Ituraea. He ruled from 4 B.C. to A.D. 44, and issued coins in several denominations. (Actual size approximately 13 mm.) (Photograph courtesy of Ira and Larry Goldberg)

Right, top and bottom: Herod Agrippa ruled as King of Judaea from A.D. 37 to 44. He is remembered for the persecution of Christians and the execution of Apostle James. His prutah coins show a canopy or umbrella on the obverse and three ears of barley on the reverse. (Actual size approximately 17 mm.)

Galilee, and his brother Philip tetrarch of Ituraea and the region of Trachonitas…. (Luke 3:1)

King Herod Agrippa (A.D. 37-44)

King Herod Agrippa was the grandson of Herod the Great, and one of the best-recorded kings of ancient Israel. His life is chronicled in The Acts of the Apostles, and *Antiquities of the Jews* by Flavius Josephus. During his short time in office he issued two distinct types of coins. Bronze prutot made for Judaea in the sixth year of his reign (A.D. 42/43) are the most common. They depict an open umbrella, or royal canopy, on the obverse, and three ears of barley on the reverse; both inanimate designs in keeping with Messianic Law. A parallel issue of Agrippa's coins was made for districts of his kingdom where his portrait or other Roman devices were not offensive. All of the portrait pieces are rare and seldom met with in coin collections.

Agrippa is well known for his persecution of the early Christians, and for killing James and imprisoning Peter.

About that time King Herod (Agrippa) laid hands upon some members of the church to harm them. He had James, the brother of John, killed by the sword, and when he saw that this was pleasing to the Jews he proceeded to arrest Peter also. (Acts 12:1–3)

Herod Agrippa II (A.D. 55-95)

Herod Agrippa II issued the largest and most varied series of coins of the Herodians. Two types have his portrait. Others were issued at various mints, and in five denominations. They were made in several years and with two different dating cycles. Some have the name of Nero in the legend. Collectors find these pieces an interesting and challenging series to study and collect. All are considered to be scarce and difficult to obtain, especially in choice condition.

Agrippa II and his sister Bernice are best remembered in biblical reference by the following passage in the Acts of the Apostles 26:27–28.

COIN OF HEROD AGRIPPA II

Herod Agrippa II issued numerous different coins and denominations during his reign from A.D. 55–95, but all of them are scarce and elusive. He disregarded the Jewish prohibition of graven images and included portraits on many of his coins. (Actual size approximately 20 mm.) (Photograph courtesy Ira and Larry Goldberg)

"King Agrippa, do you believe the prophets? I know you believe." Then Agrippa said to Paul, "You will soon persuade me to be a Christian." Paul replied, "I would pray to God that sooner or later not only you but all who listen to me today might become as I am except for these chains." Then the king rose, and with him the governor and Bernice and the others who sat with them. After they had withdrawn they said to one another, "This man is doing nothing that deserves death or imprisonment" and Agrippa said to Festus, "This man could have been set free if he had not appealed to Caesar."

Herod of Chalcis (A.D. 41-48)

Herod of Chalcis was the brother of Agrippa I. He used the title "Friend of the Emperor" on his coins, and included his portrait on all issues. All of his coins are very rare. Some are undated; others are dated "year three." When this Herod died in A.D. 48, the Roman Emperor Claudius assigned the province of Chalcis to his brother-in-law, Agrippa II. Herod of Chalcis's son, Aristobulus (A.D. 57–92), was married to the infamous Salome, who earlier had danced before Herod Antipas and demanded the head of John the Baptist.

THE PROCURATORS OF JUDAEA

Herod Archelaus was banished to Vienna in 6 B.C. because of his cruelty to the Jews, and at that same time Judaea was annexed to the Roman province of Syria. Emperor Augustus then appointed Coponius to the post of prefect, or governor over Judaea. He was the first of 14 to hold the position of procurator and, with the exception of Agrippa I who reigned as king, the procurators ruled there until the First Revolt of the Jews against Rome in A.D. 66.

COINS IN THE NEW TESTAMENT

EARLY COINS OF THE PROCURATORS

Left, top and bottom: The prutah coins of Coponius, A.D. 6–9, and those of Marcus Ambibulus, A.D. 9–12, are identical in design and can be distinguished only by the date on them. Jesus would have used these coins during his childhood. (Actual size approximately 16 mm.)

Right, top and bottom: Valerius Gratus, who governed Judaea from A.D. 15–26, is not mentioned in the Bible, but his prutah coins circulated freely throughout the Holy Land. (Actual size approximately 15 mm.)

COINS IN THE NEW TESTAMENT

Coponius (A.D. 6-9)

Coponius remained in office from A.D. 6 to 9, when he was recalled to Rome. He is not mentioned in the Bible, but has been portrayed by Flavius Josephus in *Antiquities* as being embroiled in the rivalry between Jews and Samaritans that flared up again during his tenure. His coins are easily found and relatively inexpensive. They are all small bronze prutot of a single design, that of an ear of barley with inscription in Greek on one side, and a palm tree with dates on the other. Letters for the year 36 (of Augustus's reign) equate to A.D. 6.

> The Samaritan woman said to him, "How can you, a Jew, ask me, a Samaritan woman, for a drink?" (For Jews use nothing in common with Samaritans.) Jesus answered and said to her, "If you knew the gift of God and who is saying to you, 'Give me a drink,' you would have asked him and he would have given you living water." (John 4:9–10)

Marcus Ambibulus (A.D. 9-12)

Marcus Ambibulus succeeded Prefect Coponius and continued to issue coins of the same style and design. All of his coins show an ear of barley and a palm tree with two bunches of dates. His coins can be distinguished by the use of additional chronological dates for the reign of Emperor Augustus. The year 39 equals A.D. 9, 40 equates to A.D. 10, and 41 is A.D. 11. All were issued during the time that Jesus was growing up and would have been familiar to him.

> And the child grew, and waxed strong, full of wisdom; and the grace of God was in him. And his parents went every year to Jerusalem, at the solemn day of the Pasch. And when he was twelve years old, they went up into Jerusalem, according to the custom of the feast…. (Luke 2:40–42)

Valerius Gratus (A.D. 15-26)

Valerius Gratus was sent from Rome by Tiberius to succeed Annius Rufus. He was prefect for eleven years, but little is known about him or his administration. There is no mention of Gratus in the Bible although he must have been well known to all who lived in Judea at that time. His coins are bronze prutot and a single

lepton, of various designs, among which are crossed cornucopias, lilies, vines with grapes, religious vessels, and palm branches. Following the custom of the day, his name does not appear on any of his coins, which often include the name of Tiberius Caesar and dates of his reign.

Pontius Pilate (A.D. 26-36)

Pontius Pilate is by far the best known of all administrators of this time. His existence, however, is not well documented by anything other than his coins. If it were not for his coins, and the biblical account of his delivery of Jesus to be crucified, he might well have gone unnoticed by historians. His approval by the Jews must have been tarnished by his lack of understanding or concern for their custom of excluding forbidden symbols on their coins.

Pilate issued only two types of coins during his ten-year term in office. The first bronze prutah is dated year 16 (of Tiberius Caesar) and was struck in A.D. 29. It has in its design three bound ears of barley on the obverse, and the Roman sacrificial simpulum, or libation ladle, on the reverse. His second type of prutah shows an augur's wand, or lituus, on the obverse surrounded by Tiberius Caesar's name. The reverse has a date rendered in customary Greek letters indicating the year of Tiberius Caesar's reign. LIZ=17, and LIH=18. All of these are of special interest to collectors because Pilate issued them close to the year of the Crucifixion.

> When it was morning, all the chief priests and the elders of the people took counsel against Jesus to put him to death. They bound him, led him away, and handed him over to Pilate, the governor. (Matthew 27:1–2)

> So Pilate went back into the praetorium and summoned Jesus and said to him, "Are you the King of the Jews?" Jesus answered, "Do you say this on your own or have others told you about me?" Pilate answered, "I am not a Jew, am I? Your own nation and the chief priests handed you over to me. What have you done?" (John 18:33–35)

COINS OF PONTIUS PILATE

Pontius Pilate, who governed for 10 years, minted two different types of prutot in A.D. 29, 30 and 31. His role in history would have been relatively unknown it if were not for these coins and his part in the Crucifixion. (Actual size approximately 15 mm.)

COINS IN THE NEW TESTAMENT

Pilate said to them, "Then what shall I do with Jesus called Messiah?' They all said, 'Let him be crucified!" But he said, "Why? What evil has he done?" They only shouted the louder, "Let him be crucified!" When Pilate saw that he was not succeeding at all, but that a riot was breaking out instead, he took water and washed his hands in the sight of the crowd, saying, "I am innocent of this man's blood. Look to it yourselves." (Matthew 27:22–26)

When it was evening, there came a rich man from Arimathea named Joseph, who was himself a disciple of Jesus. He went to Pilate and asked for the body of Jesus; then Pilate ordered it to be handed over.
(Matthew 27:57–58)

Antonius Felix (A.D. 52-62)

Antonius Felix served under the Roman Emperor Claudius for the first two years of his prefectship, and then under Nero for his remaining term. In B.C. 54, when Britannicus ruled briefly with Nero, Felix issued a bronze prutah with the legend BPIT to recognize the young son of Claudius who was subsequently poisoned by order of Nero. The reign of Felix was oppressive but strong. It was he who caused the apostle Paul to be sentenced to prison. A passage in the New Testament refers to this governor. When Paul was transferred to Caesarea from Jerusalem for his protection, a message was prepared to explain the mission:

And he wrote a letter after this manner: "Claudius Lysias unto the most excellent governor Felix, I send greeting."

Apparently Antonius Felix was not above accepting a bribe, as revealed in Acts 24:26, concerning the imprisonment of St. Paul.

He hoped also that money should have been given him of Paul, that he might loose him, wherefore he sent for him the oftener, and communed with him.

The coins of Felix consist of two different types of bronze prutot. Those under the authority of Claudius show crossed palm branches, while those made under Nero/Britannicus have crossed shields and spears. Both issues are dated year 14 of the reign of Caesar.

Porcius Festus (A.D. 59-62)

Porcius Festus held the procuratorship under Nero for only about one year. He issued bronze prutot with the date LE (year 5), which equals A.D. 59, and Nero's name on the reverse. Paul was tried by Felix, but he was brought for judgment before Festus, who sent him to Rome. Paul was a Roman citizen and therefore was privileged to be tried and judged there. After two years in prison, Nero had Paul put to death. When Porcius Festus died in A.D. 61/62, Nero sent Albinus to succeed him. Reference to Festus is made in Acts 24:27 as follows:

But after two years, Porcius Festus came into Felix' room; and Felix, willing to show the Jews a pleasure, left Paul bound.

COINS IN THE NEW TESTAMENT

COINS OF THE
LATER PROCURATORS

Left and middle: The Apostle Paul was sentenced to prison by Antonius Felix, who served under Claudius in A.D. 52–54, and later under Nero in A.D. 54–62. Two different styles of prutah were made to recognize his Roman allegiances. (Actual size approximately 17 mm.)

Right: Porcius Festus issued this bronze prutah in A.D. 59, near the time when he sentenced Paul to prison in Rome. (Actual size approximately 18 mm.)

CHAPTER 6

FIRST-CENTURY MONEY AND TRADE

FIRST-CENTURY MONEY AND TRADE

Life in the first century A.D. was vastly different than it is today, and yet many things were so similar that any one of us could still survive under the same conditions. People of that time worked, played, paid taxes, married, raised children, and worshiped all in their own distinctive ways. Understanding the environment and modes of that time gives a fuller and more colorful perspective to the lives of the people portrayed in the Bible, and clearer meaning to the incidents described in the New Testament.

A large number of different kinds of coins was used during that period from the birth of Christ to the time that biblical accounts were finalized in written form. Jesus, the apostles, and all of the participants chronicled in the Bible were familiar with money and commerce of the time. They saw and used the very same coins that we know today as ancient remainders of the past. Coins that have been passed down to us stand as testimony to the historical accuracy of the Bible.

There can be little doubt that money was important to every level of society in biblical times. It is mentioned in one of the most often repeated passages, that of 1 Timothy 6:10, which reads as follows: "For the love of money is the root of every evil." This is also one of the most often misquoted passages, frequently rendered incorrectly as "Money is the root of all evil."

Food, a very real necessity of life, is mentioned 124 times throughout the Bible. Money, in one form or another, is mentioned 129 times, while gold (at 417) and silver (at 282) rank even higher. Even more indicative of the significance of money in the lives of everyone is the fact that 16 of the 40 parables preached by Jesus mention coins or money.

Numerous passages in the works of the Apostles speak about money and its role in society. Among those are Matthew 18:23–35; 20:1–16; 25:14–30; and Luke 10:30–37; 12:16–21; 15:8–10; 16:1–13; 18:10–14; 19:11–27. A typical example deals with interest, and the responsibility of using money wisely and dutifully.

And it came to pass on his arrival back again having received the kingdom, that he desired those bondmen to whom he gave the money to be called to him, in order that he might know what every one had gained by trading. And did you not give my money to the bank; and I should have received it, at my coming, with interest? (Luke 19:15, 23)

Trade in Bible times evolved largely from an agrarian and barter system to a much more sophisticated international system of commerce. Palestine was well suited for both land and sea trade routes; thus, by New Testament days, foreign trade and local businesses were subject to strict regulations. In Old Testament times, Israelite farmers were poor and generally produced only enough for their own needs. As markets and a demand for local products grew, tradesmen became important to the community, and merchants set up business stalls in the city.

Money that was in use throughout New Testament Bible lands consisted of foreign coins that flowed into the region from their export of olive oil, linens, and trade goods. Coinage of Egypt, Macedonia, Phoenicia, and neighboring districts were all familiar to the Israelites because they were made on the Greek standard that closely followed the shekel in weight. Roman coins were also in daily use, and important for payments to the Roman authorities. Those coins also had a relationship to Jewish standards. The Roman denarius was equal in weight to one-quarter shekel of silver.

In addition to the use of international coins, the small bronze lepta and prutot that had been made by the Hasmonian and Herodian rulers were still in circulation, and were in great demand for use in the Temple. One of the functions of the moneychangers was to convert "heathen" money to more acceptable Jewish coins for use as offerings. Their fee for making the conversion was usually eight percent.

Hasmonean prutot of the Helenistic period, from 134 to 40 B.C., were valued at 168 to one drachma, or one-quarter shekel. Prutot of the Herodian period, 40 B.C. to A.D. 6, were valued at 96 to the Roman denarius that was also equal to one-quarter shekel. In the Roman period, from A.D. 6 to the time of the First Jewish Revolt in A.D. 66, one denarius equaled 64 prutot.

FIRST-CENTURY MONEY AND TRADE

ANCIENT COINS OF INTERNATIONAL TRADE

Left, top and bottom: Macedonia. Philip III, c. 325 B.C., silver drachm with head of Hercules on the obverse, and Zeus seated on the reverse. These coins circulated widely and were the weight of one-quarter shekel. (Actual size approximately 17 mm.)

Middle, top and bottom: Roman didrachm, c. 225–215, an unusual denomination that was soon replaced by the denarius. It was equal to a half-shekel. (Actual size approximately 21 mm.)

Right, top and bottom: Coinage of Alexandria in Roman Egypt circulated widely throughout Palestine. This silver tetradrachm of Tiberius was minted in A.D. 21 and circulated during the lifetime of Jesus. It shows the images of both Augustus and Tiberius. (Actual size approximately 27 mm.)

AUGUSTUS
Emperor from
14 B.C.–A.D. 14

TIBERIUS
Emperor from
A.D. 14–37

CALIGULA
Emperor from
A.D. 37–41

CLAUDIUS
Emperor from
A.D. 41–54

NERO
Emperor from
A.D. 54–68

Working people of that time could earn approximately one denarius, or one-quarter shekel, a day for their work. That was standard pay for laborers, fishermen, and soldiers, and was enough to provide for the living expenses of a middle-class family. Skilled craftsmen were able to earn more, but there were very few opportunities other than for tailors, bakers, scribes, builders, and pottery makers. Joseph, who is described as being a carpenter, would probably have taught his son the same trade and lived a comfortable life.

> And coming into his own country, he taught them in their synagogues, so that they wondered and said: "How came this man by this wisdom and miracles? Is not this the carpenter's son? Is not his mother called Mary…." (Matthew 13:54–55)

Roman coins in use during the first century A.D. included gold, silver, copper, and brass pieces of several denominations that were made by each of the emperors who had jurisdiction over their provinces. These would have been familiar to all who were part of Bible history, and to those who later recorded the events. Through these coins we not only have a record of Roman emperors who lived at that time, but also know what they looked like through the images on their money.

Roman emperors who issued such coins from the birth of Jesus to the end of the first century, when the final book of the New Testament was written, can be seen on the sidebars of pages 66 through 68. (Actual sizes range from 20 mm to 30 mm.)

Throughout this time both Jews and Christians were often subjected to the wrath and cruelty of the Roman rulers who sought to impart their own religion on everyone under their control. Nero was particularly harsh, and when much of Rome was destroyed during the great fire of A.D. 64, he blamed and punished the Christians for the disaster.

COST OF LIVING

Raising a family was as challenging in biblical times as it is today. Providing for food and shelter, paying taxes, and seeing that males were educated or apprenticed to a family business were all obligations for a husband. A sum of money called the *mohar* had to be paid to the bride's father by the bridegroom before marriage. If necessary it could be paid in part in the form of work by the man, but the value of the mohar was returned to the daughter on the death of her parents, or if her husband died. The girl's father, in return for the mohar, gave her husband a wedding gift, or dowry, that might be in the form of money, servants, land, or property.

At the wedding ceremony, rings or bracelets were sometimes exchanged in a simple civil ceremony before two witnesses. The bride usually wore a veil, and jewelry that included a traditional headband of ten coins. The ceremony was then followed by a wedding feast at the home of the bridegroom, or his parents. All are familiar customs that are continued today in many parts of the world.

The marriage in Cana of Galilee is described in John 2:1–11. It was a large affair attended by Jesus, his mother, and several disciples. When the supply of wine ran low, Mary asked her son to intercede; he then performed the first of his miracles by turning water into wine. The incident shows not only the high regard that Jesus had for marriage, but the significance of customs and importance of wine at that time. It was a commodity of value, necessity, and tradition.

There are few references to the cost of goods and services during the life of Jesus, but some can be found in the New Testament, the Talmud, and the writings of Josephus. Daniel Sperber's book *Roman Palestine Money and Prices* gives many citations detailing wages and prices of that period. A loaf of bread, the staple midday lunch that was usually eaten with olives or fruit, cost one-eighth of a denarius. A full meal, including wine, was probably less than one denarius. A small amphora of wine, likely imported from Chios, also cost one denarius. Rent was about four denarii per month. The cost of some necessary religious offerings was equally modest.

Are not two sparrows sold for a small coin? Yet not one of them falls to the ground without your Father's knowledge. (Matthew 10:29)

Are not five sparrows sold for two small coins? Yet not one of them has escaped the notice of God. (Luke 12:6)

In the King James translation of these accounts, the word "farthing" is used to express the denomination of the coins involved in these examples. The farthing was the smallest English coin familiar to readers of the King James text. Other translations use the word "assarion," a small Greek bronze coin that was equivalent to the Roman "as" and worth about 1/16 of a denarius. The original Latin text uses the words "asse" and "dipundio," indicating similar denominations.

GALBA
Emperor from
A.D. 68–69

OTHO
Emperor in
A.D. 69

VITELLIUS
Emperor in
A.D. 69

VESPASIAN
Emperor from
A.D. 69–79

TITUS
Emperor from
A.D. 79–81

DOMITIAN
Emperor from
A.D. 81–96

NERVA
Emperor from
A.D. 96–98

TRAJAN
Emperor from
A.D. 98–117

Jews were obligated to pay three different taxes. That due to the Roman emperors was at times used for the upkeep of heathen temples, and was offensive. Those who collected the tax were despised because of their ruthless insistence on payment. Roman money in the form of silver denarii was the usual form of payment.

The Redemption from Priesthood tax was a religious tax, as was the temple tax that was used for temple repairs and other religious purposes. Jews everywhere, whether or not they lived in the land of Israel, were required to pay the annual one-half shekel temple tax. Exodus 30:13–15 references this tax as follows:

"Every man age 20 or older paid a tax of a half shekel for the support of the tabernacle worship."

COINS OF ROMAN PALESTINE

Left, top and bottom: Roman Emperor Nero issued this tetradrachm for use in Antioch and neighboring districts. It is dated year 10, which equates to A.D. 64, the year of the great fire that destroyed much of Rome. (Actual size approximately 25 mm.)

Middle, top and bottom: Chios, first century B.C. Bronze "assarion" with a sphinx seated on the obverse and a wine jar, called an amphora, on the reverse. A coin identified as a "farthing" in the King James Bible. (Actual size approximately 18 mm.)

Right, top and bottom: Silver coins of Tyre were the only money acceptable in the Temple for payment of religious obligations. Didrachms showing the head of Melkart, and an eagle, were equivalent to one-half shekel. (Actual size approximately 21 mm.)

CHAPTER 7

PARABLES, LESSONS, AND COINS

PARABLES, LESSONS, AND COINS

Jesus frequently used stories about coins to emphasize a moral issue or describe some familiar situation. One of the most memorable of these parables concerns the laborers in a vineyard. The original Latin reference to the payment of a denarius a day for the workers gives confirmation of the standard wages of that time.

LABORERS IN THE VINEYARD

The kingdom of heaven is like a landowner who went out early in the morning to hire laborers for his vineyard. After agreeing with them for a denarius a day, he sent them into his vineyard. Going out about nine o'clock, he saw others standing idle in the marketplace, and he said to them, "You too go into my vineyard, and I will give you what is just."

So they went. And again he went out again around noon, and around three o'clock, and did as before. Going out about five o'clock, he found others standing around, and said to them, "Why do you stand here idle all day?" They answered, "Because no one has hired us." He said to them, "You too go into my vineyard." When it was evening the owner of the vineyard said to his steward, "Call the laborers and give them their wages, beginning with the last and ending with the first."

When those who had started about five o'clock came, each received a denarius. So when the first came, they thought that they would receive more, but they also received each his denarius. And on receiving it they began to grumbled against the landowner, saying, "These last ones worked only one hour, and you have made them equal to us, who bore the day's burden and the heat." He said to one of them in reply, "My friend, I am not cheating you. Did you not agree with me for a denarius? Take what is yours and go." (Matthew 20:1–15)

Another reference to the familiarity of the Roman silver denarius in Jesus' time is found in the following passage, "A certain money-lender had two debtors; the one owed five hundred denarii, the other fifty. As they had no means of paying, he forgave them both" (Luke 7:41–42). In this story, the creditor was a kind-hearted money-lender who forgave two debtors, and was rewarded by their love and appreciation. The incident was extraordinary because it must have been a very unusual occurrence.

Luke recounts a very different story that Jesus preached when he spoke against hypocrisy and covetousness in another passage. In this, he mentions the "mite," the smallest coin in use at that time, and most likely a bronze lepton of the old Hasmonean era.

And when thou art going with thy opponent to the ruler, take pains to be quit of him on the way; lest he deliver thee to the judge, and the judge to the officer, and the officer cast thee into prison. I say to thee, thou wilt not come out from it until thou hast paid the very last mite. (Luke 12:58–59)

A DAY'S WAGES AND THE LOST COIN

Above: Roman silver denarius, A.D. 130, with head of Roma on the obverse and Jupiter in a quadriga on the reverse. The standard wages for a full day's work was one denarius. (Actual size approximately 19 mm.)

Below: The mystery of the "lost coin" can be explained in understanding that the piece was part of a wedding headband and precious to the woman who lost it. Greek silver drachma coins and Roman denarii were often used for this custom. (Actual size approximately 18 mm.)

THE LOST COIN

Some of the best-known parables have meanings that are not immediately recognized because they involve unfamiliar customs. The story of the "lost coin" is a classic example. In its simplest form, the woman who lost her coin would be expected to rejoice when it was found. But why would she call her friends together to celebrate with her? The answer lies in understanding why she was concerned with the loss.

Or what woman, having ten drachmas, if she loses one drachma, does not light a lamp and sweep the house and search carefully until she finds it? And when she has found it, she calls together her friends and neighbors, saying, "Rejoice with me, for I have found the drachma that I had lost." (Luke 15:7–10)

PARABLES, LESSONS, AND COINS

"HE GAVE THEM TEN GOLD PIECES..."

Parables speak of the use of money in various ways. The gold coins cited in the Parable of the Gold Pieces, as recorded by Luke, were possibly Greek staters of Alexander the Great, or Roman aurei of Augustus or Tiberius worth 25 denarii each.

A certain nobleman went into a far country to obtain for himself a kingdom and then return. And having summoned ten of his servants, he gave them ten gold pieces and said to them, "Trade till I come." (Luke 19:12–13)

But as that servant went out, he met one of his fellow-servants who owed him a hundred denarii, and he laid hold of him and throttled him, saying, "Pay what you owe." (Matthew 18:28–30)

Why was this ointment not sold for three hundred denarii, and given to the poor? (John 12:5)

Above: Large transactions usually involved gold coins similar to the staters of Philip II (359–336 B.C.) that show the head of Apollo and a racing chariot. (Actual size approximately 18 mm.)

PARABLES, LESSONS, AND COINS

The key to more fully appreciating this parable is in the number of coins that the woman had. The specific number of ten drachma coins is a reference to the headband that the woman wore to signify that she was married. It would have been a symbol equal to today's wedding ring, and precious to her for many reasons beyond its monetary value.

Ten Greek drachmas were the equivalent of ten denarii or ten days' pay—and a considerable sum of money—but beyond that, if a woman were found guilty of infidelity, one or more of the coins could be removed from the headband. In this story the unfortunate woman who lost one of the coins was embarrassed to face her neighbors and friends for fear of being accused of adultery.

The use of Greek drachms on the bridal headband was an old tradition for showing wealth and stability. It is a custom that has been used, with modifications, in some countries ever since. In ancient times, Roman silver denarii were used when the older Greek coins were not available. The coins were usually pierced with a nail and sewn onto the headband.

THE GOOD SAMARITAN

The denarius was mentioned in several other parables that confirm its familiarity to those who listened to the moral lessons that Jesus taught. The story of the Good Samaritan was especially significant because of the animosity that usually existed between the Samaritans and the Jews.

A certain man was going down from Jerusalem to Jericho, and he fell in with robbers, who after both stripping him and beating him went their way, leaving him half-dead. But, as it happened, a certain priest was going down the same way; and when he saw him, he passed by. And likewise a Levite also, when he was near the place and saw him, passed by. But a certain Samaritan as he journeyed came upon him, and seeing him, was moved with compas-

sion. And he went up to him and bound up his wounds, pouring on oil and wine. And setting him on his own beast, he brought him to an inn and took care of him. And the next day he took out two denarii and gave them to the innkeeper. (Luke 10:30–35)

MONEYCHANGERS IN THE TEMPLE

And Jesus entered the temple of God, and cast out all those who were selling and buying in the temple, and he overturned the tables of the money-changers and the seats of those who sold the doves. And he said to them, "It is written, My house shall be called a house of prayer (Isaiah 56:7; Jeremiah 7:11); but you have made it a den of thieves." (Matthew 21:12–13)

And he found in the Temple those who were selling oxen and sheep and doves, and the moneychangers seated. (John 2:14)

This famous parable concerns the habit of merchants setting up stalls in the outer court of the Temple. There they sold sacrificial animals, and offered to change "heathen" money into the acceptable Tyrian shekels and minor copper coins of the old Hasmonian rulers.

Mosaic Law forbade charging interest on loans to fellow Jews, but the moneychangers took advantage of their unique position by adding a fee of about eight percent for their services.

They have taken gifts in thee to shed blood: thou has taken usury and increase, and covetously oppressed thy neighbors: and then has forgotten me, says the Lord God. (Ezechiel 22:12)

"HEATHEN" COIN

Moneychangers in the Temple converted "heathen" money to acceptable Tyrian and Maccabbean coins. The fee for their services was seen as an offense to the pious Jews. A silver tetradrachm of Ptolemy III, c. 230 B.C., showing the king's image, would have been converted to a similar piece from Tyre. (Actual size approximately 28 mm.)

PARABLES, LESSONS, AND COINS

Take not usury of him nor more than you have given: fear thy God, that thy brother may live with thee. (Leviticus 25:36)

THE WIDOW'S MITE

And Jesus sat down opposite the treasury, and observed how the crowd were putting money into the treasury; and many rich people were putting in large sums. And there came one poor widow, and she put in two mites, which make a quadrans. And he called his disciples together, and said to them, "Amen I say to you, this poor widow has put in more than all those who have been putting money into the treasury. For they all have put in out of their abundance; but she out of her want has put in all that she had—all that she had to live on." (Mark 12:41–44)

But looking up he saw the rich who were putting their gifts into the treasury. And he saw also a certain poor widow putting in two mites. And he said, "Truly I say to you, this poor widow has put in more than all." (Luke 21:1–4)

In these famous parables, the poor widow contributes what is described as two "mites." All accounts emphasize that the mite was the smallest bronze coin in use at that time, and although there is no

coin known by that name, it is logical to assume that the passage refers to the tiny lepta from the time of Alexander Jannaeus. Although those coins were made approximately 100 years earlier, they were still being used in the temple as offerings. Lepta of Jannaeus were the smallest of all Hasmonean coins, and the most plentiful in ancient times just as they still are today. Collectors treasure them because they are so closely connected to a biblical incident, and so readily available.

According to this parable, each of the two lepta was worth one-half of a Roman quadrans. There were 64 quadrans to the denarius, and thus her total offering was about equivalent to 1/128 of a day's wages. The miniscule sum was more than she could afford and offers a poignant lesson in charity.

THE COIN IN THE FISH'S MOUTH

And when they had come to Capharnum, those who were collecting the didrachma came to Peter, and said, "Does your Master not pay the didrachma?" He said, "Yes." But when he had entered the house, Jesus spoke first, saying, "What dost thou think, Simon? From whom do the kings of the earth receive tribute or customs; from their own sons, or from others?" And he said, "From others." Jesus said to him, "The sons then are exempt. But that we may not give offense to them, go to the sea and cast a hook, and take the first fish that comes up. And opening its mouth thou wilt find a stater; take that and give it to them for me and for thee." (Matthew 17:23–26)

The money mentioned in the Latin rendition of this parable is more exacting than that of the usual translations. In the King James Version, and other accounts, we find the coin referred to as "a piece of money." All agree that the coin retrieved from the fish was the size of a tetradrachm, or shekel, because that was the necessary amount to pay the tax for two people. The term "stater" referred to a Greek coin that was approximately equal to the tetradrachm, and twice the value of the tax that was a half-shekel. The single coin in the fish's mouth would have paid for both Jesus and Peter.

Finding such a coin in the mouth of a fish was miraculous, but not unnatural. Perhaps it was a variety of the African Mouthbrooder. They have the unusual habit of holding eggs in their mouth for protection during incubation. It could have been a natural instinct for such a fish to retrieve a shiny lost coin and hold it in its mouth.

THE TRIBUTE PENNY

Then the Pharisees went and took counsel how they might trap him in his talk. And they sent to him their disciples, with the Herodians, saying, "Master, we know that thou art truthful, and that thou teachest the way of God in truth and that thou carest

WIDOW'S MITE AND THE COIN IN THE FISH'S MOUTH

Left, top and bottom: Coins that the poor widow gave to the Temple were small lepta, or "mites," that represented much of her sustenance. (Actual size approximately 28 mm.)

Right, top and bottom: Jesus found money for tribute in a most unlikely place: a fish's mouth. The coin must have been a tetradrachm of Tyre, the exact amount needed to pay the tax for Peter and himself. (Actual size approximately 13 mm.)

PARABLES, LESSONS, AND COINS

naught for any man; for thou dost not regard the person of men. Tell us, therefore, what dost thou think: Is it lawful to give tribute to Caesar, or not?" But Jesus, knowing their wickedness, said "Why do you test me, you hypocrites? Show me the coin of the tribute." So they offered him a denarius. Then Jesus said to them, "Whose are this image and the inscription?" They said to him, "Caesar's." Then he said to them, "Render, therefore, to Caesar the things that are Caesar's, and to God the things that are God's." And hearing this they marveled, and leaving him went off.

(Matthew 22:15–22)

A corresponding translation reads:

"Is it lawful to pay the census tax to Caesar or not? Should we pay or should we not pay?" Knowing their hypocrisy he said to them, "Why are you testing me? Bring me a denarius to look at." They brought one to him and he said to them, "Whose image and inscription is this?" They replied to him, "Caesar's." So Jesus said to them, "Repay to Caesar what belongs to Caesar and to God what belongs to God." [Other versions refer to "a Roman coin," or a "penny."]

The question, the answer, and the moral of this story seem simple and clear. Even the coin that is mentioned is easy to identify when it is called a denarius. The Roman census tax at that time was one denarius, the equivalent of one day's pay. The King James Bible uses the word "penny" in place of denarius. The transliteration was meant to make the word more understandable to 16th century readers who were familiar with the English form of money, where a silver penny was approximately the

same size as the old Roman silver coin. Throughout the years this story has become so well known that the Roman denarius of Tiberius has become widely known as "the Tribute Penny."

It seems likely that the coin involved was indeed a Roman silver denarius of Emperor Tiberius. He ruled from A.D. 14 to 37, during the lifetime of Jesus, and his coins would have been in use throughout Judaea at that time. They would also have been required for payment of the census or tax. They have an image of Emperor Tiberius, who was known as Caesar, and an inscription giving his name. A similar coin of Caesar Augustus who ruled from 14 B.C. to A.D. 14 could also have been used, but there is widespread accord about the coin of Tiberius being the specific piece.

As straightforward as this story seems, it has much deeper significance than is at first apparent. The Herodians who accompanied the Pharisees were there to see if Jesus would be disloyal to his obligation to pay the Roman tax. If he did, he surely would have been accused of being an enemy of Rome. The Pharisees were there to see if Jesus would betray his Jewish allegiance. Either answer, it seemed, would alienate him to one or the other. It was a trap from which, they believed, he could not escape.

The answer that Jesus gave to his adversaries was brilliant and disarming. "Repay to Caesar what belongs to him,"—that is, those who willingly used Caesar's coins should repay him in kind. The answer avoided taking sides in the question of the lawfulness of the tax. Those who hypocritically asked about duty to the law of God were told to be concerned with what is due to God.

CAESAR'S TRIBUTE PENNY

When the Pharisees attempted to trap Jesus into betraying his duty to God or to Caesar, he called for a denarius to show that it was issued by Caesar. Such coins show a portrait of the Roman emperor on the obverse, and his mother Livia on the reverse. (Actual size approximately 20 mm.)

CHAPTER 8

COINS AND THE PASSION

COINS AND THE PASSION

THIRTY PIECES OF SILVER

The term "pieces of silver" is used many times in the Bible in reference to coins that were equivalent in weight to the shekel. The tetradrachms of Tyre were coins that had been approved for use as offerings in the Temple, and were the most commonly available coins in use throughout the Holy Land. They were relatively large coins for that time, and had a value of nearly four days pay. Although these coins contained only about a half ounce of silver, we must remember that ancient coins had a purchasing power far greater than today, and a single shekel was considered to be a significant sum of money.

> If the ox gore a bondman or a handmaid, he shall give to their master thirty shekels of silver, and the ox shall be stoned.
> (Exodus 21:32)

> And when the Madianite merchants passed by, they drew him out of the pit, and sold him to the Ismaelites, for twenty pieces of silver, and they led him into Egypt. (Genesis 37:28)

> And I bought her to me for fifteen pieces of silver, and for a core of barley, and for half a core of barley. (Osee 3:2)

> Then was fulfilled that which was spoken by Jeremias the prophet, saying: And they took the thirty pieces of silver, the price of him that was prized, whom they prized of the children of Israel. (Matthew 27:9)

These examples confirm that there were established prices for a life in ancient times. A fixed "blood-price" was not without precedent. Many cultures throughout time have set similar standards for practical purposes. The custom seems more sophisticated than the current practice of arbitrarily placing the value in millions of dollars, as seen in some lawsuits.

The price that was agreed upon for the betrayal of Jesus was the usual price of a life taken by accident or that of a slave being sold into captivity. It would equate to about 20 days' pay, or approximately what one would spend for a month's living expenses. There could be no justification for any amount of money given in exchange for such a life, but in that time and place, it was a standard price.

> Then one of the Twelve, called Judas Iscariot, went to the chief priests, and said to them, "What are you willing to give me for delivering him to you?" And they assigned him thirty pieces of silver. And from then on he sought out an opportunity to betray him. (Matthew 26:15–16)

> Then Judas, who delivered him up, seeing that he had been condemned, filled with remorse, returned the thirty pieces of silver to the chief priests and the elders. And having cast down the pieces of silver in the Temple, he left the place, and went away and hanged himself. And the chief priests took the pieces of silver and said, "It is not lawful to cast them into the Corban, since it is the price of blood." (Matthew 27:3, 5–6)

There is no doubt that the coins given to Judas Iscariot were shekels from the Phoenician city of Tyre. A few other coins of the same weight could have been included in the payment, because they were not intended to be used in the Temple, but the availability of the Tyrian coins makes them the number one candidate for this momentous transaction.

Tyrian coins were accepted by the Jewish community despite their depiction of an eagle and a foreign god. The obverse of these coins shows the head of Melkart with a lion's skin around his neck, and a laurel wreath on his head. He was a Phoenician god, who is shown posing in the form of the Greek god Herakles. On the reverse is an eagle standing on the prow of a ship, carrying a palm under its right wing. In the field are letters and symbols indicating the date in which these coins were minted from 126/125 B.C. to the time of the First Revolt of the Jews against Rome.

PONTIUS PILATE

The betrayal, crucifixion, and death of Jesus are related in Matthew 27, and John 18. Pontius Pilate becomes a central figure in this scenario, where the arrest and trial of Jesus is described in some detail.

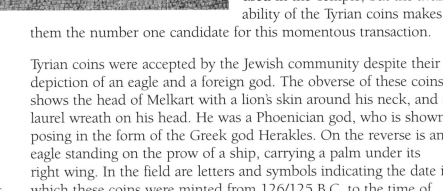

> Pilate therefore went outside to them, and said, "What accusation do you bring against this man?" They said to him in answer, "If he were not a criminal we should not have handed him over to you." Pilate therefore said to them, "Take him yourselves, and judge him according to your law." The Jews, then said to him, "It is not lawful for us to put anyone to death." (John 18:29–31)

COINS OF THE BETRAYAL

Left, top and bottom: Judas Iscariot agreed to betray Jesus for 30 pieces of silver. The coins were quite likely tetradrachms of Tyre that had recently been made in Jerusalem, similar to this one minted in A.D. 10. The amount was a considerable sum in purchasing power at the time. (Actual size approximately 26 mm.)

Middle, top and bottom: Some of the bronze lepta coins of Pontius Pilate were minted in years close to the Crucifixion. The exact date of the event is not known for certain, but could have been the year 17 of Pilate's coins, or A.D. 30. (Actual size approximately 15 mm.)

Right, top and bottom: Soldiers were bribed to deny that Jesus had risen from the tomb on the first Easter Morning. A gold aureus (equal to 25 silver denarii) of Roman Emperor Tiberius might have been part of the payment. The design on these coins was the same as on his denarii. (Actual size approximately 20 mm.)

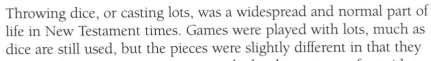

COINS AND THE PASSION

Pilate was a minor administrator who might well have been forgotten if it was not for his involvement in the trial of Jesus. He is mentioned in the New Testament, but the only other solid evidence of his existence lies in the two kinds of coins that he minted in years near to the Crucifixion. One of them is dated LIZ (year 17), indicating A.D. 30, and possibly the year that Jesus died. The others were made in the years 16 and 18. Pilate's coins are bronze prutot, and the two designs that were used both bear the name of the emperor Tiberius Caesar rather than that of Pilate.

Pilate said to them, "Then what shall I do with Jesus called Messiah?" They all said, "Let him be crucified!" But he said, "Why? What evil has he done?" They only shouted the louder, "Let him be crucified!" When Pilate saw that he was not succeeding at all, but that a riot was breaking out instead, he took water and washed his hands in the sight of the crowd, saying, "I am innocent of this man's blood. Look to it yourselves." And the whole people said in reply, "His blood be upon us and upon our children". Then he released Barabbas to them, but after he had Jesus scourged, he handed him over to be crucified. (Matthew 27:22–26)

CASTING LOTS FOR HIS GARMENTS

The soldiers therefore, when they had crucified him, took his garments and divided them into four shares, a share for each soldier. They also took his tunic, but the tunic was seamless, woven in one piece from the top down. So they said to one another, "Let us not tear it, but cast lots for it to see whose it will be," in order that the passage of scripture might be fulfilled: "they divided my garments among them, and for my vesture they cast lots." This is what the soldiers did. (John 19:23–24)

And after they had crucified him, they divided his garments, casting lots, that it might be fulfilled which was spoken by the prophet, saying: "They divided my garments among them; and upon my vesture they cast lots." (Matthew 27:35)

Throwing dice, or casting lots, was a widespread and normal part of life in New Testament times. Games were played with lots, much as dice are still used, but the pieces were slightly different in that they were marked only on two or four sides. The six-sided pieces used now are a more recent innovation, but the lots were otherwise similar in size and shape. They were made of either bone or wood, or cast in bronze.

The contest played by the soldiers at the Crucifixion of Jesus, as recorded by John and Matthew, was a game of some sort that used Roman dice. This would have been in favor of simply "matching coins" which was another favorite pastime of the soldiers. If bronze pieces were used, they were just as valuable as coins because all metal items were highly prized at that time. The large Roman copper shipbuilder's nails that may have been used at the Crucifixion would also have been as valuable as money.

SOLDIERS AT THE TOMB

When Jesus was laid to rest in the tomb, Roman soldiers were posted there to guard against the body being stolen, so that the disciples could say their Lord had risen. An account of the Resurrection is given in the gospels of Matthew, Mark, Luke, and John. All are in accord about the holy women carrying spices to the sepulcher before dawn, and reaching it after sunrise; they are anxious about the heavy stone, but know nothing of the official guard. In Matthew 28:2–4, an angel frightens the guards, puts them to flight, and rolls away the stone.

Now while they were going, behold, some of the guard came into the city and reported to the chief priests all that had happened. And when they had assembled with the elders and had consulted together, they gave much money to the soldiers, telling them, "Say, his disciples came by night and stole him while we were sleeping. And if the procurator hears of this, we will persuade him and keep you out of trouble." And they took the money, and did as they were instructed. (Matthew 28:11–15)

The money that the soldiers received as a bribe for their silence has been described as a large sum, indicating that the coins might have been either Tyrian shekels, or perhaps a Roman gold aureus of Emperor Tiberius.

ROMAN "LOTS" DICE
AND CRUCIFIXION NAILS

Left: Roman dice called "lots" were cast by soldiers to divide the garments of Jesus. The worth of each piece was inscribed in circles. (Actual size approximately 12 mm.)

Right: Large Roman copper shipbuilder's nails were sometimes used to affix criminals to a post or cross in the torturous execution known as crucifixion. (Actual size approximately 95 mm.)

CHAPTER 9

THE BEGINNING OF CHRISTIANITY

THE BEGINNING OF CHRISTIANITY

In the first few decades after the Death and Resurrection of Jesus, the spread of Christianity was a slow and painful transition. The Apostles and disciples preached the word about him through their travels and writing. Their accounts of his miracles and deeds were eventually recorded and compiled in the form now known as the New Testament. Efforts to establish and promote the new religion met with resistance from many quarters, but none more violent and abusive than from the emperors of Rome.

Under the disciples' leadership, many people in Jerusalem became followers of Jesus, and in towns and villages all over Palestine, new groups of believers were established. One of the earliest converts was a Pharisee named Saul, who was later known as Paul. He had been a fierce opponent of the new sect, but was miraculously changed when he went to arrest believers in Damascus. About the same time, a Roman centurion named Cornelius also became a notable convert to the new way of life.

In Antioch, the capital of the province of Syria, many people became believers, and it was there that they were first called Christians. It was from Antioch that Paul and Barnabas traveled to Cyprus (in Turkey) in A.D. 45 or 46, to preach the Gospel. There, many non-Jews as well as Jews became followers of the new faith. This development sparked a controversy as to whether non-Jews could be accepted into the religion. In a conference held at Jerusalem in A.D. 49, decisions were made to welcome all converts, and to curtail the involvement of non-Jews in keeping traditional Jewish rituals.

As the new religion grew and solidified, efforts were made to spread the word of Christ as far as possible. Paul made missionary journeys into Europe, and by A.D. 64 there were churches in all the main centers of the Roman Empire. The city of Antioch became the major hub of the new Christian church.

It was during this period that opposition to change became manifest in Rome and Jerusalem. Herod Agrippa, the grandson of Herod the Great, was educated in Rome, and was a friend of Caligula and Claudius. Strongly pro-Jewish, he persecuted the Christians, had James killed, and imprisoned Peter. The procurator Antonius Felix, who served under Claudius in A.D. 53 to 54, and under Nero A.D. 55 to 62, caused the apostle Paul to be sentenced to prison at Caesarea. Under Nero, in Rome, the situation was even worse—thousands of Christians were savagely killed for sport and entertainment. The old legend that Nero "fiddled" while Rome burned is based on his dedication to the arts; he often dressed in the robes of Apollo and played the lyre or recited poetry. One of his copper coins made near the time of the great fire of Rome in A.D. 64 (which he blamed on the Christians) shows him in such a performance.

VESPASIAN'S INSULTS

Top: Vespasian quelled the Jewish uprising in Jerusalem in A.D. 70, and issued many coins to commemorate his victory. A typical design shows Judaea seated beneath a trophy with the legend "Judaea Capta." (Actual size approximately 19 mm.)

Bottom: One of the most detested victory coins of Vespasian is a denarius showing a pig and piglets on the reverse, as an insult to the Jews. (Actual size approximately 19 mm.)

REVOLTS OF THE JEWS AGAINST ROME

The excesses of Nero also extended to Jerusalem, where his oppression of the Jews caused a major revolt in A.D. 66. In 67, Nero appointed Vespasian, a skillful military leader, to quell the rebellion. He was proclaimed Emperor of Rome soon after Nero's death, and his eldest son Titus successfully ended the war in A.D. 70. Vespasian's victories in Jerusalem afforded him a military distinction that was reflected in his coinage, which often depicted the defeated Jews with the inscription JUDAEA CAPTA. Some of his insulting coins also show a sow with piglets, the insignia of the 10th Legion sent to Jerusalem to quell the uprising. Upon Vespasian's deathbed, he is reported to have said, "Alas, I think I am becoming a god." Soon after, the Senate deified him, but the honor was more akin to sainthood than the actual elevation to a god's status.

COINS OF TWO
IMPERIAL PERSECUTORS

Left, top and bottom: Roman Emperor Claudius, A.D. 42–43, who is shown on the obverse of this bronze coin called an "as," with Minerva on the reverse, was an early persecutor of the Christians. (Actual size approximately 30 mm.)

Right, top and bottom: The early Church suffered under the rule of Emperor Nero, who blamed the Christians for starting the fire that destroyed much of Rome in A.D. 64. He is shown on one of his coins playing the lyre. (Actual size approximately 30 mm.)

THE BEGINNING OF CHRISTIANITY

THE BEGINNING OF CHRISTIANITY

Throughout the revolution that lasted from A.D. 66 to 70, a large number of purely Jewish coins were made to supply the needs of war, as offerings for the Temple, and as political or inspirational statements. These were all special coins that were made with religiously acceptable designs. The most common of these was a bronze prutah that displayed a grape leaf on one side and an amphora, or jar, on the other. The legend on these coins reads "For the freedom of Zion," and a reference to the year of issue, either year two or three of the revolution.

It was during this time that the famous Jewish shekel coins were first made. Before this, any biblical reference to a shekel indicated a weight of approximately one-half ounce, or the equivalent silver tetradrachm of Tyre, that had been authorized for use as a religious offering. The revolt gave opportunity and incentive for the Jewish leaders to issue a coin of their own that would show their independence and resolve, as well as suiting their commitment to using money without a graven image. The issuance of these Jewish coins was also necessitated by the discontinuation of old Tyrian-style shekels around A.D. 65.

The silver shekel and half-shekel coins that were produced during the period of the First Revolt share a common design, with a ceremonial cup on the obverse and three pomegranates on the reverse. The Hebrew legend on these coins contains the date (one through five), the denomination (shekel, or half-shekel, of Israel), and "Jerusalem the Holy." The silver shekels weigh approximately 14 grams, and the half-shekel coins weigh approximately 7 grams. All of these coins are thick and clumpy, with edges that have been hammered, or peened, in a technique similar to that used on some of the Syrian tetradrachms of that period.

In the devastating revolutionary war that lasted for more than four years, the Roman emperor Vespasian and his son Titus destroyed much of Jerusalem, including the Holy Temple, and killed tens of thousands of citizens. The Roman 10th and 12th legions slowly, but surely, quelled the revolt and brought the

situation back under their control. The Jewish historian Josephus recorded that the total number of prisoners taken during the war amounted to 97,000 and those who perished during the entire siege numbered more than 1,000,000. Reference to this is found in Isaiah 3:26 as follows: "And her gates shall lament and mourn, and she shall sit desolate on the ground."

BAR KOCHBA'S WAR

The Second Revolt of the Jews against Rome was under the leadership of Simon Bar Kochba. It lasted from A.D. 133 to 135 and was the occasion for minting the last Jewish coins in antiquity. The inscriptions on these coins contain the name Shimeon (Simon) and sometimes his title "Prince of Israel," and other coins of the period bear the name of "Eleazar the Priest," or simply "Jerusalem." Bar Kochba coins of the first two years were dated "Year one of the redemption of Israel," or "Year two of the freedom of Israel." During the third year and until the end of the war, the coins were undated and bore the slogan "For the freedom of Jerusalem."

The revolt of 132 was sparked by continued harassment from the Roman emperors, particularly Hadrian, who intended to rebuild Jerusalem and rename it Aelia Capitolina. He also passed laws that forbade circumcision under the penalty of death. Under the leadership of Bar Kochba, the resistance fighters made a heroic effort to oust the Romans in the hopes of rebuilding their own city and the Holy Temple that was central to their religion. In this role Bar Kochba was seen by some as the promised Messiah, and greatly revered. His name, which means "son of a star," was even foretold by prophecy. Proof of his existence, however, was only told by his coins until papyrus containing letters from him were found in the Dead Sea caves in 1960 and 1961 stating the following: "There shall step forth a star (kochba) out of Jacob, And a scepter shall rise out of Israel." (Numbers 24:17)

Coins that were minted during the Bar Kochba War were made of silver and bronze, and in many different designs. The entire issue was

---

PRUTAH AND ROMAN 10TH LEGION BRONZE

Above: A typical bronze coin of the First Revolt period has a ceremonial cup on the obverse and a vine leaf on the reverse. (Actual size approximately 17 mm.)

Below: The Roman 10th Legion was sent to Jerusalem to fight in the Jewish War. Many bronze coins were counterstamped with the Roman numeral X to indicate their presence during the sieges of Jerusalem and Masada. (Actual size approximately 29 mm.)

[90]

COINS OF THE JEWISH REVOLTS

Left, top and bottom: The famous shekel of the Bible was not an actual coin until such pieces were made by the rebelling Jews in A.D. 66–70. The design of these shekels and half-shekels shows a ceremonial cup on the obverse and three pomegranates on the reverse. (Actual size approximately 23 mm.)

Second, top and bottom: A new type of shekel, or sela, was minted during the Second Revolt from A.D. 132 to 135. These silver coins are attributed to Simon Bar Kochba, and have various dates and legends. The central image is a frontal view of the Temple. (Actual size approximately 26 mm.)

Third, top and bottom: Bronze coins of the Second Revolt were made in several different sizes and designs. The most prevalent coins show a palm tree on the obverse and a vine leaf on the reverse. (Actual size approximately 25 mm.)

Right, top and bottom: A second revolt of the Jews against the Romans occurred in A.D. 132. It was brought about by Emperor Hadrian, who enacted laws forbidding religious activities under penalty of death. His silver denarii show the emperor's portrait. (Actual size approximately 19 mm.)

overstruck on older coins that were taken from circulation around the district of Palestine. These included Roman provincial tetradrachms from Antioch, the ubiquitous Roman denarii, provincial drachmas, and local bronze city coins, mainly from Ashkelon and Gaza. It is believed that Bar Kochba possibly obtained the gentile coins needed for overstriking by means of a public loan for the war effort.

The overstriking was a means of converting offensive money into something more worthy of use by devout Jews. The new coins were also given new names: the denarius was called a zuz, and the tetradrachm, or shekel, equal to four Roman denarii, became a sela. The largest and most impressive of the Bar Kochba coins is the silver sela (shekel) that shows in its design the façade of the Temple of Jerusalem with the Ark of the Covenant and scrolls displayed inside.

After the revolt had been subdued, the Romans proceeded to build their new city on the site of Jerusalem. They named it Aelia Capitolina, and erected a temple to Jupiter. Thus, the hopes and dreams of the Jews to rebuild the Holy Temple of Jehovah were crushed, leaving behind a legacy of coins as a reminder of the glorious past.

SECOND REVOLT OVERSTRUCK COINS

Second Revolt coins, the size of a quarter-shekel or denarius, were made with many different designs related to sacred implements, grapes, and branches. All were overstruck on old Roman coins. (Actual size aprromately 19 mm.)

THE JOURNEYS OF PAUL

It was into this mixture of political and religious turmoil that Christianity attempted to gain a foothold and expand to places beyond Jerusalem. The Apostle Paul's journey in A.D. 45 took him and Barnabas from their base at Antioch in Syria by ship to Cyprus, and from there to present-day Turkey. His second journey in A.D. 48 to 51 included an 18-month stay in Corinth. All along the way new churches were established, and his teachings were recorded in writings that have come down to us as Bible text. The cities that he visited can be traced through contemporary coins in a way that captures the imagination of many collectors and brings them closer to understanding the locations and cultures of that time.

And one night the Lord said to Paul in a vision, "Do not fear, but speak and do not keep silence; because I am with thee, and no one shall attack thee or injure thee, for I have many people in this city." So he settled there a year and six months teaching the word of God among them.
(Acts of the Apostles 18:10–11)

When Paul returned to Jerusalem after his third journey, he was arrested. He spent the next two years (during A.D. 58 to 60) in prison, before appealing to be heard by the emperor. Luke accompanied him when he set sail for Rome, but this time he was under guard, and his missionary activities curtailed. In Rome, Christians came out to meet him, and for the next two years Paul continued to preach the message of Jesus, though under house arrest and awaiting trial.

By the end of the first century, Christianity had spread throughout much of the Roman Empire despite some strong opposition and persecution. Several of the Roman emperors who followed Nero were tolerant of the new religion as long as it did not interfere with their personal preference or the numerous deities that were sacred to the Romans. One notable exception was Elagabalus (218–222) who was the hereditary priest of the Syrian sun god Elagabalus. The excesses of this depraved emperor were somewhat mitigated during the reign of Philip I (244–249), who some believe was the first Roman emperor to adopt Christianity as a personal religion. It is known that his wife, Otacilia Severa, was devoted to Christianity and made pilgrimages to Antioch at the time of Easter. Coins of these historical figures are relatively common and can be easily acquired by collectors.

The last great Roman persecutor of Christians was Emperor Diocletian (A.D. 285–305). One irony of his reign is that despite his cruelty, one of his reforms—the division of the Roman Empire into districts called dioceses—continues to be employed in the organization of the Roman Catholic Church, the Anglican Communion, and other churches to the present day.

THE BEGINNING OF CHRISTIANITY

PERSECUTION
AND PROTECTION

Left, top and bottom: Elagabalus issued this bronze coin at Antioch in A.D. 218–222 for use in the Roman colonies. It has the portrait of this young man who was devoted to the sun god and tried to impose his religion on the entire empire. (Actual size approximately 25 mm.)

Middle, top and bottom: His grandmother, Julia Maesa, was far more tolerant of other religions and curtailed Christian persecution. (Actual size approximately 19 mm.)

Right, top and bottom: The last great persecutor of the early Christians was Emperor Diocletian (A.D. 285–305). He issued this bronze coin about the same time that he was issuing many harsh decrees against the Christians. (Actual size approximately 29 mm.)

ROME ACCEPTS CHRISTIANITY

The first Roman emperor to proclaim Christianity as a state religion was Constantine I, the Great (A.D. 307–337). He was not the ideal Christian, as one might expect, and in fact he murdered his wife and son. It is said that in a military campaign, in what is now Italy, he beheld in the heavens, beneath the sun, a flaming cross bearing the inscription "In hoc signo vinces" (By this sign you will conquer). The following night, the cross again appeared to him in a dream, and he was told to use this sign as his emblem. The decisive battle at the Milvian Bridge in A.D. 313 was then successful and motivated his edict that embraced the new religion. From that time forward, the Roman sun god was removed from his coins and replaced with non-religious depictions.

Constantine is reputed to have been baptized and converted to Christianity on his deathbed. Prior to that he led a life that was anything but religious, and more devoted to the Roman sun god Sol. About two years before he died, he established Sunday as the day of worship. He also moved the capital of the empire from Rome to Byzantium, and named the new city Constantinople. Throughout his life, Constantine was strongly influenced by his mother Helena, a devout Christian, who it is believed discovered the remains of the true cross upon which Jesus was crucified.

Constantine intervened in ecclesiastical affairs to achieve unity; he presided over the first ecumenical council of the church at Nicaea in 325, and he built churches in the Holy Land where his mother is credited with identifying numerous places associated with biblical events. Coins with Helena's portrait were minted by her son, but none of them show any of the religious scenes connected to her discoveries.

With the favorable conditions established by Constantine, the Christian religion grew and flourished,

not only in Rome, but throughout the Mediterranean. Various symbols, like the one adopted by Constantine, slowly began to appear on coins in place of the pagan gods that had preceded them. The most prominent of these was the familiar XP symbol known as the Christogram, or Chi-Rho monogram. The Greek letters are an abbreviation for the name Jesus Christ, and are believed to have been the emblem seen by Constantine in his vision.

For many years the XP symbol was used as part of the design on numerous coins of the Roman and Byzantine empires. When Magnentius became emperor in A.D. 350, he used the monogram as the principal design on some of his coins, even though he was not a true Christian. From then on, the only Roman emperor to shun the Christian religion was Julian II, the Apostate, who for a short period from 360 to 363 attempted to restore the old pagan Roman religions.

COINS OF THE FIRST CHRISTIAN EMPEROR

Constantine I, the Great, ruled from A.D. 307 to 337. He is considered to be the first Christian emperor of Rome, but his actions sometimes belied that thought. Some of his coins are dedicated to the sun god Sol, while others show the Christogram (XP) that was his personal religious badge. (Top, actual size approximately 21 mm. Bottom, actual size approximately 17 mm.)

THE BYZANTINE EMPIRE

Constantinople became a capital of the Roman Empire in 330 when Constantine the Great renamed the city of Byzantium after himself. It gradually developed into the true capital of the eastern Roman provinces, which included southeastern Europe and parts of southwestern Asia. Also embraced were the northeast corner of Africa, which include the present-day countries of the Balkan Peninsula, as well as Syria, Jordan, Israel, Lebanon, Cyprus, Egypt, and the eastern part of Libya.

The period of notable history encompassed by the Byzantine Empire ran from the reign of Anastasius I (491–518) to the capture of Constantinople by the Turks in 1453. The Seljuk Turks, after making devastating raids into Byzantium's eastern territories, crushed an imperial army at the Battle of Manzikert (1071) and overran most of Byzantine Asia Minor. Meanwhile, the Byzantines lost their last foothold in Italy and were alienated from the Christian West by a schism (1054)

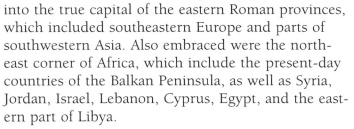

COINS OF
PHILIP AND OCTACILIA

Emperor Philip I and his wife Otacilia Severa, A.D. 244–249, were possibly the first Roman rulers to adopt the new Christian religion. Octacilia is known to have been a true believer and devoted member of the church of Antioch. (Left pair, top and bottom, actual size approximately 25 mm. Right pair, top and bottom, actual size approximately 24 mm.)

between the Orthodox Church and the Papacy. The era is noteworthy for the development of Christian practices and values, and numismatically significant for the original religious themes that were used on Byzantine coins.

The most interesting coins of this period are those with portraits of Jesus and his mother Mary. They are some of the most ancient of all images of the Holy Family, but none of them pre-dates the year 685, and all are probably imaginative representations. The standardized bust of Christ most often used is, however, the one that was widely accepted, and has continued to be used as a standard representation of Jesus in art ever since.

Few earlier images of Christ exist. The most ancient is a late third-century fresco from the cemetery of Saints Peter and Marcellinus in Rome that shows Christ with light skin, short hair, and a clean-shaven face. There is also a fourth-century sarcophagus from Rome that likewise shows him with short hair and clean-shaven. A fifth-century ivory plaque from Sicily (now in the Victoria and Albert Museum) shows the adult Christ as clean-shaven, but with long hair. As a Jew, the most likely form of hairstyle for that time would have been long hair and a full beard.

The earliest depiction of Christ in the "traditional" style used on most Byzantine coins is found on a sixth-century painted icon that depicts the nimbate (with halo) bust of Christ facing, dispensing a blessing and holding a book of gospels. He is bearded and has long, wavy hair and rather slender features. The image is strikingly similar to that used on a gold solidus of Byzantine Emperor Justinian II, made during his first reign (A.D. 685–695). In that depiction, a cross set behind the head replaces the nimbus, but the similarity is unmistakable.

During the second reign of Justinian (705–711), a different image of Christ is used. This one, for which there is still no explanation, depicts a shaven man with short curly hair. Use of the Christ-image was short lived at this time because of the impending iconoclastic movement that

sought to suppress all religious images. At the Seventh Ecumenical Council of Constantinople in A.D. 754, the Church declared that such representations would no longer be tolerated:

Supported by the Holy Scriptures and the Fathers, we declare unanimously, in the name of the Holy Trinity, that there shall be rejected and removed and cursed out of the Christian Church every likeness which is made out of any material and color whatever by the evil art of painters.

The General Council of approximately 350 bishops at Nicaea reversed the unfortunate decree in A.D. 787, but not before many of the ancient depictions of Jesus, and perhaps other Bible figures, were destroyed and lost forever. The coins of Justinian II are among the few remaining early images of Christ, and the only icons generally available for public appreciation outside of museums. His gold coins are scarce and valuable, but fortunately for collectors, the imagery was revised in later years and used on many gold and bronze coins that are regularly available.

With the death of Emperor Theophilus in 842, the iconoclast controversy ended, and Michael III reinstated the Christ-image on his gold coins. Then followed a period that lasted until the end of the Empire when various Christian images appeared on the vast majority of Byzantine coins.

Interest in collecting Byzantine coins has grown noticeably since 1970, but prices for nice coins are still relatively low when compared to the older Greek and Roman coins. The major hindrance to forming an amiable collection is in the poor appearance of these coins, which are usually well worn. Most Byzantine copper coins tend to suffer from years of circulation, repetitive designs, poor minting techniques, and inferior artistry. Yet, these coins are some of the most interesting and deserve to be collected for their historical aspects as well as their Christian imagery.

MAGNENTIUS AND JULIAN II COINS

Above: Emperor Magnentius issued the first coin with a design devoted exclusively to Christianity with this bronze double centenionalis of A.D. 350. Although an avowed Christian, Magnentius also restored certain rights to the pagans. (Actual size approximately 27 mm.)

Below: The last Roman emperor to strenuously resist the new religion was Julian II, A.D. 360–363, who wanted to restore polytheism. His large bronze coins depict a cult bull. (Actual size approximately 26 mm.)

COINS WITH BIBLICAL THEMES

GREEK AND
BYZANTINE ANGEL COINS

Left, top and bottom: Winged figures come in many forms. The ancient Greeks, in 485 B.C., showed Nike flying overhead to announce victory to a chariot race. (Actual size approximately 26 mm.)

Right, top and bottom: Emperor Constantine I changed the image to that of an angel on his coins in the fourth century A.D. It was used many times thereafter on Byzantine coins similar to the gold solidus of Focus, A.D. 602–610. (Actual size approximately 21 mm.)

COINS WITH BIBLICAL THEMES

ANCIENT GOD OF ISRAEL

The earliest depiction of the God of Israel may be found on a very unlikely coin of Phoenicia that was possibly minted around 350 B.C. Little is known about this coin, which was unknown until a unique specimen was discovered and in time became the subject of intense study in 1934. Researchers concluded that the inscription on the mysterious coin could be a reference to the Persian name for Jehovah. The image on the coins shows a bearded deity seated on a winged wheel and holding a falcon. The remarkable design is interpreted as being a representation of God as visualized by the Persian rulers of Judaea.

A bearded god enthroned with an eagle on his hand had long been a common art-type of Zeus, and the winged wheel had been used to represent the sun. It follows, then, that this coin represents Jehovah under the guise of a solar Zeus. Thus, a connection was formed between the principal god of the Greek pantheon and the God of Israel. This imagery was further strengthened throughout the years when Christian artisans depicted God as a bearded father figure identical to Zeus as seen on countless ancient coins. The transition from Nike to angel, and from Zeus to Jehovah was a simple adjustment for the art world. With no Jewish images to guide them, any depiction was as believable and valid as any other. Coins alone now give us the oldest record of the origin of these images, and how they came to be accepted as realistic depictions of the unknown and unseen.

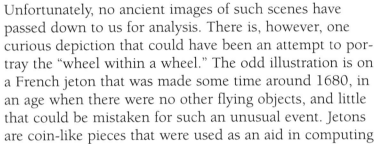

THE GOD OF ISRAEL

The God of Israel, as visualized by the Persians, is depicted on this fourth century B.C. coin in the form of a seated figure holding a falcon. (Photograph courtesy of the British Museum)

EZEKIEL'S VISION

Now it came to pass in the thirteenth year, in the fourth month, on the fifth day of the month, when I was in the midst of the captives by the river of Chobar, the heavens were opened, and I saw the visions of God. (Ezekiel 1:1)

And I saw, and behold a whirlwind came out of the north: a great cloud, and a fire enfolding it, and brightness was about it: and out of the midst thereof, that is, out of the midst of the fire, as it were the resemblance of amber. And in the midst thereof the likeness of four living creatures: and this was their appearance: there was the likeness of a man in them. (Ezekiel 1:4–5)

The four "living creatures" described in this Old Testament account have been loosely explained as being cherubim of strange shapes that supported the throne of God, and, as it were, drawing his chariot. This entire chapter appeared so obscure and so full of mysteries to the ancient Hebrews that no one was allowed to read it before they were 30 years old. The entire account of Ezekiel's experience is so mesmerizing that it has been explained by some as a true spiritual vision, and by others as the appearance of extra-terrestrial visitors in a space ship. His description of a "wheel within a wheel," and creatures with wings, may well have been an attempt to portray mechanical devices at a time when such things were inconceivable.

Unfortunately, no ancient images of such scenes have passed down to us for analysis. There is, however, one curious depiction that could have been an attempt to portray the "wheel within a wheel." The odd illustration is on a French jeton that was made some time around 1680, in an age when there were no other flying objects, and little that could be mistaken for such an unusual event. Jetons are coin-like pieces that were used as an aid in computing sums by people who had to figure mathematical equations by Roman numerals. The jeton was both a counter (the name survives in most stores today) and a teaching aid that sometimes included the alphabet or a scene from the Bible.

The strange (unidentified) flying object that is shown on the French jeton on page 103 looks enough like the modern concept of a UFO to be taken for one. And it may well be, if it is indeed not the famous wheel described by Ezekiel when he wrote the enigmatic account of his vision sometime around 590 B.C. Whatever it is, the object shown on this piece is as mysterious as Ezekiel's narrative.

NOAH'S ARK

And God remembered Noah, and all the living creatures, and all the cattle that were with him in the ark, and brought a wind upon the earth, and the waters were abated. (Genesis 8:1)

The story of a disastrous and far-reaching flood is as old as recorded history. It appears in many cultures around the world, in oral and written accounts, as a morality story. In Genesis the flood prompted Noah to provide a safe haven for his family and

COINS WITH BIBLICAL THEMES

EZEKIEL'S "WHEEL"?

The mysterious object shown on this French jeton of c. 1680 may be Ezekiel's "wheel," or a UFO. Perhaps they were both the same kind of extraterrestrial visitation. (Actual size approximately 27 mm.)

COINS WITH BIBLICAL THEMES

the other creatures to be saved. The end of the catastrophic event was announced by the returning of a freed dove carrying an olive branch. God then promise that the world would never again be destroyed by a flood, and set a rainbow to signify this. Both signs have remained forever as symbols of tranquility and peace on earth.

In numismatics, the flood was recorded on at least two rare ancient coins. Both have similar scenes showing Noah and his wife alighting from the ark. On one, the box-like ark is inscribed with the name "Noah," leaving no doubt as to the meaning of the scene. A dove with an olive branch is flying above the ark, on these coins that were made during the reigns of the Roman emperors Macrinus (in A.D. 217 to 118) and Philip Sr. (in A.D. 244 to 249). These two coins are the only ancient pieces that depict biblical scenes, and both were made in Phrygia (modern-day Turkey, not far from Mount Ararat), where the original ark is believed to have landed.

THE HOLY TEMPLE OF JERUSALEM

No depiction of the Holy Temple as restored by Herod was made until long after it had been destroyed by the Romans in A.D. 70. There are descriptions of both the first and second temples of Jerusalem, but the only image is that shown on the silver sela (shekel) coins minted during the Bar Kochba War of A.D. 133 to 135. These coins show a frontal view of the temple with the Ark of the Covenant within its portals. This holy object, along with many other sacred items, had been stored in the temple ever since the time of the Babylon captivity. All of those sacred objects were lost when the temple was destroyed by the Romans during the time of the First Jewish Revolt.

When Roman forces again captured Jerusalem in A.D. 135, the Temple Mount was made into a sanctuary for Zeus, and Jews were forbidden to enter the city under penalty of death. The image of the Holy Temple seen on the silver shekels of Bar Kochba remain as

important visuals of the place where Mary made her offering for the redemption of Jesus (Luke 2:22,24), and where Jesus is known to have taught nearly 2,000 years ago.

THE SAINTS

Numerous coins have been dedicated to saints of the church. A few were authorized by saints, and one was actually made by an important saint. Collecting coins of the saints is an intriguing adjunct to any interest in the numismatic record of Christianity throughout the ages. In addition to coins associated with the saints, numerous medals, badges, and commemorative pieces have been made throughout the years as souvenirs and religious symbols. Unlike the coins, however, the commemoratives did not share any direct connection to the saints while they were living. The following are some of the persons who had tangible numismatic associations.

Saint Helena

Saint Helena was converted to Christianity late in life. She was the mother of Constantine the Great, and used her high position and wealth in the service of her new adopted religion. She helped build churches throughout the empire, and nearing age 80 led a goodwill tour of the Holy Land where she reputedly discovered the True Cross and other religious artifacts. Her portrait can be seen on Roman coins made periodically by her son Emperor Constantine I (c. A.D. 318 to 329) and during, and shortly after, her lifetime by her three grandsons.

Pope Saint Zacharias

Pope Saint Zacharias (or Zachary) was a pious man who is best known for spending his personal fortune to free slaves and for many other good deeds. He ruled wisely and well as an early pope of the Church from A.D. 741 to 752, and was the first pope to issue money in his own name. Coins that have been attributed to him are small copper pieces that are extremely rare, and might have been intended for use as tokens of unknown value.

COINS WITH BIBLICAL THEMES

TWO OLD TESTAMENT SUBJECTS

Left: The catastrophic flood is the only biblical event specifically shown on an ancient coin. The event is recorded by a depiction of Noah's ark on this large Roman bronze coin of Macrinus, A.D. 217–218. (Actual size approximately 35 mm.) (Photograph courtesy of Kerry Wetterstorm)

Right: The Ark of the Covenant can be seen within the portal of the Holy Temple on the shekels of Bar Kochba minted in A.D. 133–135, during the Second Revolt. (Actual size approximately 26 mm.)

Edmund of East Anglia

Edmund of East Anglia is also known as Edmund the Martyr. He ruled as king of Danish East Anglia from A.D. 855 until his death in 870. He was a model ruler and concerned with justice for his subjects. Following one of a series of armed engagements with invading Danes, he was captured and ordered to give his Christian people to the pagan invaders; he refused and was beaten, whipped, shot with arrows, and beheaded. Silver pennies were issued by Saint Edmund during his lifetime. A similar memorial coinage was made shortly after his death, by King Aethelred I.

Saint Stephen

Saint Stephen of Hungary was born pagan but baptized with his father at age 10. He ruled as king of the Magyars in Hungary from 1001 to 1038. He married Saint Gisela, sister of Emperor Saint Henry II. Saint Astricus served as his advisor. Known as Stephen the Great, he founded monasteries and organized dioceses throughout his kingdom. The father of Saint Emeric, he engaged Saint Gerard Sageredo to tutor his son. The small silver denar coins issued by Saint Stephen are scarce, but relatively available to collectors.

Louis IX

Louis IX, who was also known as Louis Capet, ruled as king of France from 1226 to 1270. He founded monasteries, built leper hospitals, and collected relics. Saint Louis has been called the Patron of the Crusades because of his dedication to the cause. He personally led two crusades, and died on the second. During the reign of Saint Louis IX, large silver coins, known as *gros tournois*, were issued in France, and small silver pieces were made for use by the crusaders.

Saint Eligius

Saint Eligius is famous as being the Patron Saint of Coin Collectors. He is also known as Eligius of Noyon; Eloi; and Eloy. As a young man he was apprenticed to the master of the mint at Limoges, and later was appointed to that same position under King Clotaire II at Paris. He was noted for his piety, hard work, and honesty. Eligius was a skillful metalworker who produced gold coins for Clothaire, Dogobert I, and Clovis II, prior to 639 when he then entered the priesthood and became bishop of Noyon. The coins designed by Eligius usually bore the king's bust on the obverse and a cross or monogram on the reverse. Sometimes Eligius's name was added to identify his work. Mintage of his tiny gold coins was always limited, and very few of these rare pieces have survived.

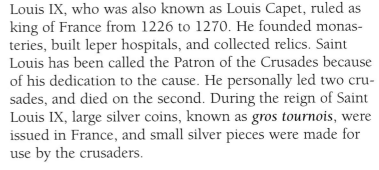
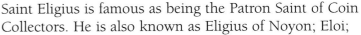

SAINTS LOUIS, ELIGIUS, AND EDMUND

Above: Edmund, King of East Anglia, was proclaimed a saint after he was killed by the Vikings who were invading England. Silver pennies with his name were made during his reign from 855 to 870. (Actual size approximately 20 mm.) (Photograph courtesy of Lawrence Stack)

Middle: The Patron Saint of Numismatics, Saint Eligius, was an actual minter who struck gold coins for French kings prior to A.D. 639. (Actual size approximately 12 mm.) (Photograph courtesy of Johns Hopkins University Numismatic Collection)

Bottom: Louis IX, King of France (1226–1270), was made a saint, in part because of his involvement in two crusades. Coins in his name were made for France and the crusaders. (Actual size approximately 25 mm.)

COINS WITH BIBLICAL THEMES

A GALLERY OF SAINTLY COINS

Left, top and bottom: Helena, mother of Constantine the Great, was converted to Christianity and made pilgrimages to the Holy Land where she reputedly discovered many holy relics. Her image can be is seen on Roman bronze coins minted c. A.D. 326. (Actual size approximately 19 mm.)

Middle, top and bottom: Saint Zacharias was the first pope to issue coins. He made small bronze tokens sometime around A.D. 750. (Actual size approximately 15 mm.)

Right, top and bottom: Saint Stephen of Hungary ruled as king from 1001 to 1038, during which time he issued small silver denars with his name and title. (Actual size approximately 18 mm.)

CHAPTER 11

COLLECTING BIBLICAL COINS

COLLECTING BIBLICAL COINS

Among the many other coins associated with biblical history are pieces with images of the saints, apostles, and the Holy Family. One of the most charming shows the Annunciation and depicts an angel carrying the message to Mary. The Kings of Naples made both gold and silver versions of these coins in 1266 to 1285. Another very popular piece was issued for use in Ireland sometime around 1665, and later shipped to America for circulation in New Jersey in 1682. These coins show an image of Saint Patrick on one side, and King David playing a harp on the other.

The Nativity is recorded on some medieval coins, as are popes, bishops and other clergy. England's King James, who ordered the translation of the Bible that now bears his name, issued coins throughout his reign from 1603 to 1625. The silver pennies that he made were similar in size to the Roman denarius mentioned in the Bible, and the reason that the denomination was substituted in the King James Version.

Less than delightful scenes on some other coins and medals from around the world show the Crucifixion, and in the case of coins made by the Knights of Jerusalem (1307 to 1798), the head of John the Baptist on a platter.

In addition to the many interesting and collectible genuine coins associated with the Bible, there are many souvenirs, replicas, and outright forgeries of these same coins. Some have been made to deceive, but most are intended to serve as reminders of the past. Imitations of ancient Jewish coins have been made for sale to pilgrims and tourists to the Holy Land for hundreds of years. Most are imitations of the shekel coins that were made during the first and second revolts of the Jews against Rome. The vast variety of these "false shekels," and the great age of some of these pieces, has made them valuable collectibles in their own right. All replicas that have been made since 1973 are subject to the United State Hobby Protection Act, and must be impressed with the work "COPY" in large letters to prevent them from being sold as genuine.

Replicas that are made for educational purposes can be an entertaining and valuable adjunct to the study of Bible history, but they must not be confused with genuine coins that are scarce and valuable historical documents. Nothing can equal the thrill of holding a genuine coin that passed in trade among the very people who lived during biblical times.

Determining whether ancient coins are genuine or replicas is something best left to numismatists (and scholars). Yet, the fact that counterfeits do exist should not deter anyone from collecting biblical coins. Professional dealers who trade in ancient coins are experts in detecting false pieces and carefully avoid offering such things for sale. Even a minimum amount of experience in handling ancient coins can usually give a collector confidence in detecting those odd pieces that are "just not right." Buying coins from street vendors in ancient lands is always chancy and is not recommended for any but those most experienced in detecting false coins.

Authentication of old coins often depends on knowing how the genuine pieces were made in ancient times. The process was simple, but not unlike the way coins are made today. A blank of precious metal was prepared, and pressed between two hard metal dies. The image that was carved on the dies was then transferred to the coin. The entire operation, of course, was done by hand in ancient times, rather than by the various mechanical methods of later days.

In the earliest period of coinage, during the seventh and sixth centuries B.C., most of the coins were made from a single engraved die, and a hand held punch. A heated lump of metal was placed on the anvil die and forced into it by a sharp blow of the punch by a hammer. The resulting coins had an image on one side and a punch mark on the reverse. The blanks of electrum, gold, or silver that were used were prepared by casting molten metal in a mold.

Coinage methods evolved to a more sophisticated level when the ancients began using two engraved dies to stamp both sides of each coin. The hand-hammering process continued to be used for centuries thereafter, but over the years the quality of artistry waxed and waned according to the modes of the time. It was not until the mid-16th century that a mechanical screw press was first used to augment hand power for the striking of coins. The single exception to making coins by the ancient hand-hammering method was an early experiment by the Romans when their largest copper pieces were cast in molds during the period from about 270 to 200 B.C.

FRENCH, IRISH, AND ENGLISH COINS

Left, top and bottom: The Annunciation, with Archangel Gabriel and Mary, is depicted on this silver "carlino" of Charles II, Count of Anjou, made c. 1300. (Actual size approximately 20 mm.)

Middle, top and bottom: Saint Patrick is the principal figure on these copper coins that were used in Ireland and colonial America c. 1682. (Actual size approximately 26 mm.)

Right, top and bottom: King James of England ordered the Bible translation that bears his name. The term "penny" was used to identify the Roman denarius because of its similar size. (Actual size approximately 17 mm.)

HOLDING HISTORY IN YOUR HANDS

The study and collecting of ancient coins related to the Bible is a fascinating hobby. It is something that appeals to many people who may have only a casual acquaintance with obsolete coins, but are interested in learning more about the Bible. It appeals to Bible scholars who have wondered about the names and descriptions of the money and people discussed in the Gospels. Collecting appeals to everyone who has ever longed for a physical or vicarious connection with the past. Collecting these artifacts not only brings people close to ancient times, it broadens their knowledge of many obscure aspects of the Bible.

Relics of the past can usually only be seen in museums. In the case of coins, we are fortunate that they are plentiful enough to be available at modest prices for those who seek them. Many of the pieces described in this book can still be purchased at remarkably reasonable prices because they have been found in large numbers, and are

available through many sources. Each year hundreds of "widow's mites" reach the market from new finds in the Holy Land, and even some of the scarcer large silver coins continue to be unearthed with some regularity. As remarkable as it seems, genuine ancient coins of Bible times have survived until today, and are still available to collectors and students, as well as for the great museums of the world.

Many resources are available to those who would pursue the hobby of collecting coins of the Bible. Descriptions of ancient coins and information about current values may be found in numerous books and catalogs. Any public library is a likely starting place to find related books on the subject. Searching the Internet will provide numerous sites dedicated to ancient coins, and some specifically dedicated to biblical coins. There you will also find numerous other related historical resources that add to the understanding and enjoyment of the miracle of the Bible and its messages, which are still as important today as they were in the past.

THE WIDOW'S MITE AND FALSE SHEKELS

Above: Tiny "widow's mite" coins are still plentiful enough to be available at very modest prices. (Actual size approximately 12 mm.)

Below: False shekels have been made for many years for sale to Holy Land tourists. Most have imaginative designs that are not at all like the original coins. (Actual size approximately 30 mm.)

INDEX

Index of Bible Verses